Somerset & Dorset Sunset

MICHAEL WELCH

Capital Transport

ISBN 978-1-85414-323-5

Published by
Capital Transport Publishing
P.O. Box 250, Harrow, HA3 5ZH

Printed by
CS Graphics
Singapore

Front cover: One of Somerset's most famous landmarks, the 520 foot Glastonbury Tor, stands out in the background as the 7.10pm Highbridge to Evercreech Junction 'all stations' train sets off from its Glastonbury & Street station stop on 5th August 1961. On this particular day the train had started at Burnham-on-Sea for the benefit of people who had spent a day out at the seaside. The motive power is a rather elderly former S&D Class 3F 0-6-0, No.43216, which was built by Neilson & Co. Ltd, in September 1902. This engine survived to become the last representative of the ex-S&D locomotives in traffic and was eventually withdrawn in September 1962. *David Soggee*

Back Cover: Bulleid Pacific locomotives Nos. 34006 *Bude* and 34057 *Biggin Hill* get into their stride as they head away from Midford with an LCGB special run to commemorate closure of the S&D line. The S&D was never an easy line to operate due to its fierce gradients, severe curvature on some sections and three separate sections of single track. Tight curves on this stretch of the line – note the very tight bend in this shot – precluded any fast running and south of Radstock the gradients had the same effect! *Michael Chown*

Title page: Trains on the S&D made four crossings of the river Stour, the last for northbound trains being just north of Sturminster Newton. Here, a morning Bournemouth to Templecombe train, hauled by an unidentified BR Standard Class 4MT 2-6-4T, crosses the river's placid waters and momentarily disturbs the peace and tranquillity of this truly delightful location. This shot was taken on the penultimate day of S&D passenger services, 4th March 1966. *Charles Whetmath*

Introduction

During the first weekend of March 1966 the roads in certain parts of Somerset and Dorset were unusually busy. Cars could be observed racing along normally quiet country lanes and figures festooned with cameras and tape recorders seen hurrying up muddy farm tracks and across fields. The local populace could be forgiven for thinking that, such was the excitement, aliens had just landed from another planet or gold had been discovered in the nearby hills. But those in the know knew exactly what was causing all the fuss – it was the final weekend of services on the much loved Somerset & Dorset (S&D) line and hundreds of people from many parts of Great Britain had come to photograph and travel over the line before it was closed forever on Monday 7th March.

The history of the route has been very well documented over the years so, perhaps, only a reasonably brief outline is appropriate here in case there are readers unfamiliar with the line's past. The very first section of (what later became) the S&D line was opened to public traffic by the broad gauge Somerset Central Railway (SCR) from Highbridge to Glastonbury on 28th August 1854. Branches from Highbridge to Burnham-on-Sea and Glastonbury to Wells followed in 1858 and 1859 respectively. The Dorset Central Railway's (DCR) standard gauge line from Wimborne to Blandford opened on 1st November 1860. The next major milestone in the development of the S&D line occurred on 3rd February 1862 when the SCR opened its extension from Glastonbury to Cole (near Bruton) where it met the DCR's line from Templecombe. The two lines amalgamated later the same year to form the Somerset & Dorset Railway. When the missing link from Templecombe to Blandford came into use on 31st August 1863 through running from Wimborne to Burnham-on-Sea became possible, the SCR line being converted to mixed gauge. The route was wholly standard gauge by 1870. The promoters hoped that substantial traffic would be attracted to their line, which connected the English Channel with the Bristol Channel, but when this did not materialise they decided to gamble everything on an extension from Evercreech to Bath to connect with the mighty Midland Railway. This steeply graded and highly scenic route, opened on 20th July 1874, altered the whole character of the S&D line which overnight became an important route linking the North of England and Midlands with the South Coast. The Bath Extension, as the new line was called, also passed through the North Somerset coalfield which became a major source of revenue for the S&D. The cost of construction brought about the financial collapse of the Somerset & Dorset Company, however, which was leased to the Midland and London & South Western railways as equal partners in a joint committee. In 1885 a link was opened between Corfe Mullen and Broadstone obviating the need for time-consuming reversals at Wimborne. After the Grouping in 1923 the line still managed to retain its independent and distinctive character, and even in the line's twilight years the fire buckets at Midford still bore the initials 'S&DJR'.

In more recent years the S&D achieved what has been described as only a 'modest usefulness'. Examination of the summer 1957 timetable reveals that on Mondays to Fridays a decidedly thin service of only five through trains was advertised between Bath and Bournemouth, though it should be pointed out that additional stopping services were provided and the frequency of the service south of Templecombe was reasonable. It should also be borne in mind that in the 1950s private car ownership was still the preserve of the better off and the masses still relied on public transport to a considerable degree. The principal train of the day was, almost needless to say, the famous 'Pines Express' which was a long distance through working with a restaurant car connecting Manchester and Bournemouth. This long-standing service first ran in 1910, the name being introduced in September 1927. On summer Saturdays the S&D line, which usually had a relaxed and unhurried air, suddenly came to life and was extremely busy with packed holiday trains from the north of England and the Midlands to the South Coast. The density of traffic was such that the route's three single line sections, and long steep gradients, were bottlenecks that caused the operating authorities endless headaches on top of the perennial problem of finding sufficient serviceable locomotives to power the trains! Most of the northbound trains ran in the morning and the southbound in the afternoon, but if relief trains to the north were scheduled to leave Bournemouth after lunchtime pathways on the single line sections were hard to find among the succession of southbound services and delays could soon occur. On the freight side coal traffic was buoyant at the northern end of the route and there was considerable stone traffic from various quarries in the Mendip Hills. Milk trains ran from dairies at Bason Bridge, on the Highbridge branch, Wincanton and Bailey Gate. In addition there was the general freight traffic, such as farm produce, that was associated with a predominately rural area.

It is widely considered that the beginning of the end for the S&D came in February 1958 when the entire line north of Henstridge (except for Templecombe station) was placed under the control of BR's Western Region (WR). Later it also gained control of an additional stretch southwards to Blandford Forum and the entire Salisbury to Exeter line. The run-down of the S&D commenced soon afterwards when the beer traffic from Burton-on-Trent, which had run over the line since it was opened, was re-routed via Taunton. Other through freight trains ceased to run, including an Avonmouth to Blandford fertiliser train which was diverted to operate via Westbury in order to deprive the S&D of this traffic. In 1962 the WR made the shock announcement that the 'Pines Express', and all other long-distance inter-regional services, would be re-routed to run via Oxford, thus dramatically reducing the line in status to little more than an unimportant rural branch. Since taking over the WR had sought to remove as much traffic as possible from the route, so it probably came as no surprise to many when it was tabled for closure in the Beeching Report published in March 1963. The WR had pursued a relentless policy aimed at reducing the line to a totally uneconomic condition, thus making the case for closure unassailable. On 7th September 1964 the last remaining night freights and 2.40am mail train from Bath to Bournemouth were withdrawn, and the line closed at night for the first time since the 1870s. The unpainted stations, which once had immaculate waiting rooms and neatly manicured flower beds, were a pitiful sight; abandoned goods yards and derelict signal boxes added to the sense of neglect. On 10th September 1965 the Government announced their consent to closure, despite previous assurances that no major closures would be sanctioned pending a thorough review of transport policy. Doubtless, many people had feared the worst but, even so, it must have come as a hammer blow to the many conscientious and loyal staff who had given the best years of their lives to the line they loved. An improved, more economical diesel-operated service might well have saved the line from closure and this failure to make the service more attractive infuriated countless staff who felt betrayed by the WR management. After a flurry of farewell special trains the S&D, a line of immense character for which so many people had a special affection, was laid to rest on the night of 6th March 1966. The stirring sound of a heavy freight battling up to Masbury summit and echoing across the Mendip Hills would no longer be heard.

Compiling this album has been a hugely enjoyable experience and I am deeply grateful to all of the photographers who have kindly made their irreplaceable transparencies available for publication. In addition, Chris Evans, David Fakes, John Langford and Graham Mallinson have read through the manuscript and suggested many worthwhile corrections and improvements to the text. Slides from the collection of the late R.C. Riley have been kindly provided by Rodney Lissenden. Thanks are also due to Roger Merry-Price for providing historical information. I accept responsibility for any errors that have remained undetected.

M.S.W.
Burgess Hill,
West Sussex,
April 2008

Dedication
As this book was about to go to print the death was announced of Charles Whetmath, some of whose pictures are featured in this publication. Charles was a professional railwayman for 45 years, an accomplished photographer and for many years served the Great Western Society, latterly as their publicity officer. His photographic collection has been bequeathed to that organisation for future generations to enjoy.

Contents

It is arguable whether Bath (Green Park) station should be included in a book about the S&D because it was actually constructed by the Midland Railway (MR) which regarded the ten miles-long branch from Mangotsfield to Bath as an important addition to its far-flung network. The station, which opened on 4th August 1869, was designed by J.C. Crossley who, no doubt with the architectural magnificence of the city in mind, produced an elegant station with a Georgian frontage built in Bath stone. There was an attractive classical façade with Ionic columns and a balustraded parapet. S&D trains used the station from 20th July 1874 when the Bath Extension opened. Known as the 'Midland Station' for many years, it was officially renamed Bath (Green Park) in 1951 and for many years the canopy nameboard proclaimed 'LMS and S&D Station'. This interior view of the premises shows the train shed's arched glass roof which ran for about half the length of the platforms. This photograph was taken on 3rd April 1965. *Roy Denison*

A further picture of Bath (Green Park) station showing Ivatt Class 2MT 2-6-2T No.41243 simmering at Platform Two on 4th July 1959. Officially Platform One was classed as the departure platform whilst Platform Two was regarded as the arrival line, but in reality they were both signalled in either direction. Unfortunately, neither could accommodate the long summer holiday trains that became such a feature of operations. The southernmost of them, Platform One, could only hold nine bogie carriages whilst the other one accommodated a mere eight coaches. The layout was constrained by the river Avon, the tracks crossing the river on two parallel cross-braced iron girder bridges. Green Park was actually a four-road station, the two centre tracks being used for running round and coach stabling. Following closure the station deteriorated alarmingly but in 1971 it gained listed building status and a year later Bath City Council purchased the site. In 1981 restoration commenced in connection with the development of a retail store and the beautifully restored station and train shed were formally opened in December 1982. Only the trains were missing, alas! *R. C. Riley*

In a scene perhaps more reminiscent of Bedford, Burton-on-Trent or Skipton sheds a quartet of Class 4F 0-6-0s clusters around the turntable at Bath (Green Park) shed on 3rd May 1959 while a Class 2P 4-4-0 is partially visible on the right of the picture. It is difficult to believe that this picture was taken quite deep in the West Country! The locomotives are standing outside the two-road, former MR shed, which was accessed from a 60-foot turntable. The stone-built MR shed was on a slightly higher level than the S&D shed building. The vintage coach body, on the right, was used by Bath enginemen for their mutual improvement classes. *Trevor Owen*

The four-road S&D shed at Bath was largely built of wood with a timber trussed roof, something of an architectural curiosity, perhaps, among railway locomotive sheds. Not surprisingly, it had a propensity to ignite(!) but the ever-vigilant staff always managed to extinguish any conflagration that occurred. The shed could accommodate up to eighteen engines. In this illustration of the shed's interior LMSR 'Jinty' 0-6-0T No.47276 and GWR pannier tank engine No.3758 are visible. This picture was taken on 6th March 1966 and both machines were stored out of use awaiting removal for scrapping. In September 1965 Green Park station was used for filming 'The Wrong Box' and No.47276, partly repainted light green, featured in some of the sequences. *Trevor Owen*

A possibly unwelcome interloper at Bath (Green Park) station! Photographed back in the days when the authorities took a much more tolerant attitude to people wandering about on the permanent way, a rail tour waits at Green Park station's Platform One on 7th June 1964. A 'Castle' Class 4-6-0, No.7023, *Penrice Castle*, provides the motive power. It is unlikely, however, that the arrival of a locomotive designed by the Great Western Railway (it was actually built by BR in June 1949) would have met with the universal approval of the S&D staff at Green Park, bearing in mind the rivalry between the two companies. The locomotive was powering the last leg of a Home Counties Railway Society tour from London which covered the entire S&D system, including the Highbridge branch, before returning to the capital from Bath via Gloucester and Stroud. The cramped site of the station due to its close proximity to the river is evident in this picture. *Michael Chown*

The driver of the 1.10pm stopping train to Templecombe already has his locomotive's tablet catching arm extended to collect the single-line token at Bath Junction as the train gets underway from Green Park station on 21st March 1964. Part of the roof of the former S&D locomotive shed can just be discerned on the left of the shot. The four-road building was constructed of wood, unlike the more substantial nearby MR building which was built of stone. The locomotive depicted is BR Standard Class 5MT 4-6-0 No.73049, which had received a general overhaul at Eastleigh Works six months previously and was repainted in fully lined out green livery. Bath Station signal box is on the right of the picture. *Hugh Ballantyne*

A scene at Bath Junction, where the former MR line to Mangotsfield diverged from the S&D route, showing Stanier Class 5MT No.44945, which is in quite clean condition, getting into its stride with the relief to the northbound 'Pines Express' on 26th May 1962. The train seems to be largely made up of LMSR-designed rolling stock. On the left a couple of locomotives can just be seen simmering on Bath shed. In the 1950s a number of Stanier 'Black Fives' were allocated to Bath for work over the S&D line and their ranks included No.44945 at one time, so it must have been something of a homecoming for this locomotive! At the time of this picture it was based at Saltley shed in Birmingham, so may have been a regular visitor. *Hugh Ballantyne*

Another illustration of a Stanier 'Black Five', or at least part of it, at Bath. No.44841 waits patiently to take the train northwards as BR Standard Class 4MT No.75073, piloting rebuilt Bulleid Pacific No.34045 *Ottery St. Mary*, approaches Green Park station with the 10.05am SO Bournemouth to Bradford train on 30th June 1962. The gas holder in the background marks the site of Bath gas works which had a network of sidings and provided much business for the railway. The author could not resist including this shot because *Ottery St. Mary* used to be a Brighton-based engine prior to being rebuilt and, besides being his favourite Bulleid Pacific, was an almost daily sight at his local station. Like nearly all locomotives based there Brighton shed kept No.34045 in sparkling external order. Those were the days!
Hugh Ballantyne

Immediately after passing Bath Junction the S&D line swung away from the Midland route and turned nearly 180 degrees until it was heading in a south-easterly direction out of the city. It was also climbing all of the time on a gradient of 1 in 50 until the top of the bank was reached just inside Combe Down tunnel, around two miles from the junction. Here, BR Standard Class 4MT No.75027 and rebuilt Bulleid Pacific No.34040 *Crewkerne* exert maximum effort past Oldfield Park as they endeavour to gain as much momentum as possible for the steep climb ahead. The train is the 10.55am SO Manchester to Bournemouth West and this picture was taken on 25th August 1962. No.75027 was destined to survive until the last days of BR steam in the north-west of England and was purchased for preservation on the Bluebell Railway, in Sussex, where it remains. It is not operational at the time of writing. *Crewkerne* was not so lucky, alas, being withdrawn in July 1967, when steam on the Southern Region ended, and was eventually cut-up in March 1968. Another picture of this train, taken at Shepton Montague, appears later in the book. *Hugh Ballantyne*

BATH (GREEN PARK) TO MIDFORD

The S&D's formidable gradients, beautiful scenery and, even in its closing years, reasonable variety of motive power meant that it was an irresistible attraction for enthusiasts and many rail tours visited the line. Here, on 2nd May 1965 LMSR-designed Class 8F 2-8-0 No.48309 is depicted climbing out of Bath and approaching Devonshire tunnel with the Locomotive Club of Great Britain's 'Wessex Downsman' tour from London. A number of bystanders have gathered on Maple Grove bridge to watch the train pass by. The rooftops of Bath and distant hills provide a wonderful setting for this photograph. Devonshire tunnel (440 yards) had an unventilated and notoriously restricted bore, the clearance from the top of most locomotives' chimneys to the tunnel roof being less that a foot, so conditions on the footplate were frequently asphyxiating for engine crews, especially those of banking engines, who no doubt breathed a huge sigh of relief when they emerged into the pure, fresh air of Lyncombe Vale. Another facet of Devonshire tunnel concerned the natural springs encountered during construction and because of the volume of water a sump was built into which water constantly flowed. The water was channelled through an underground trackside pipe to Bath motive power depot, so it was not wasted. *John Beckett*

After emerging from Devonshire tunnel southbound trains, still climbing at an unrelenting 1 in 50, ran through Lyncombe Vale, a surprisingly peaceful area that was little over a mile from Bath city centre as the crow flies. They then passed through Combe Down tunnel (1,829 yards), another unventilated bore, where (as previously mentioned) the summit of the incline out of Bath was reached. After leaving Combe Down tunnel down trains entered the delightful Horsecombe Vale and crossed Tucking Mill viaduct where, on the lovely spring day of 10th April 1965, BR Standard Class 4MT 4-6-0 No.75072 is seen hauling the 4.37pm Bath to Templecombe stopping train: the tunnel mouth is hidden by trees on the left. Tucking Mill viaduct was originally built to take a single track but was doubled in 1891 when plans were mooted to lay a second track from Midford as far as Combe Down tunnel. This idea never came to fruition, however, due to the high costs involved. *Hugh Ballantyne*

A lovely portrait of Midford station, taken on 12th July 1960, with the resident signalman leaning out of the window of his tiny cabin and the Whitaker tablet-exchanging apparatus clearly visible. The station here, which was 4½ miles from Bath (Green Park), was perched on a ledge cut into the steep hillside and its cramped location restricted passenger facilities to simple, somewhat primitive, wooden buildings and an extremely narrow platform. The station was located on the single line, the 32 miles-long double track section to Templecombe beginning on Midford viaduct just beyond the southern end of the platform. The signal box may have been small, but its importance cannot be overstated as it played a crucial role in traffic regulation, particularly on busy summer Saturdays, controlling entry onto the single line section to Bath. The rather unusual signal in the middle of the picture is a backing signal. If the driver of an up train decided there was a risk of his train stalling on the 1 in 100 gradient in Combe Down tunnel he would bring his train to a halt and advise the Midford signalman on the lineside telephone. The signalman would then pull off the backing signal which authorised the driver to set back onto the up road of the double line on the viaduct, passing other signals at danger. The driver would then decide whether to 'have another go' or wait for assistance. *R.C.Riley*

For many years the first up train of the day was the 7.00am from Templecombe to Bath which is seen here rolling into Midford station on 18th August 1962. The eight-arch 168 yards-long Midford viaduct carried the railway across the B3110 Frome to Bath road, Cam Brook, the Somersetshire coal canal and the trackbed of the GWR Limpley Stoke to Camerton branch. The course of this line, which became famous following the filming of 'The Titfield Thunderbolt' in 1952, can be clearly seen. The locomotive in charge of the train is S&D Class 7F 2-8-0 No.53810 which would not have been unduly taxed hauling its modest three-coach load of Bulleid stock. Later the same day it had a much tougher assignment paired with a BR Standard Class 4MT 4-6-0 on the heavy Cleethorpes to Exmouth through train. *Colour-Rail*

The BR Standard Class 4MT 2-6-0s were a frequent sight on S&D line passenger trains, working from the Bournemouth end of the route. These locomotives were introduced to the line in the 1950s after a test run on 5th March 1955 but engines of this class were never based at an S&D shed. They continued to appear right up to the end, however, by which time some representatives of the class were in disgraceful external condition. Here, No.76009, running without its front number plate, crosses Midford viaduct with the 1.10pm Bath to Templecombe stopping train on 11th December 1965. *Michael Allen*

Many pictures have been taken at this marvellous location and the vast majority feature down trains. So, for a change, here is a shot of an up train! On Saturday 25th August 1962 the S&D line was very busy and BR Standard Class 5MT 4-6-0 No.73054, piloting Bulleid 'West Country' Pacific No.34040 *Crewkerne*, had been stopped at Midford's up inner home signal because the single line section onwards to Bath was occupied, so the photographer had time to compose his picture. The train is unidentified but, judging by the motive power, is likely to have been 'The Pines Express'. Later in the day *Crewkerne* returned southwards at the head of the 10.55am SO Manchester to Bournemouth but this time with BR Standard Class 4MT No.75027 as pilot. *Roy Hobbs*

The S&D line abounded with outstanding photographic spots and this must surely be one of the finest. The location is, almost needless to say, looking across the picturesque valley at Midford towards the station whose signal box can just be discerned. The train is 'The Pines Express' from Manchester to Bournemouth with LMSR Class 2P 4-4-0 No.40569 piloting rebuilt Bulleid 'West Country' Class Pacific No.34046 *Braunton*. This portrait is thought to have been taken on 18th July 1961. This was the final year that the 2Ps were used on piloting work over the S&D: they were replaced by BR Standard Class 4MT 4-6-0s. On Mondays to Fridays 'The Pines Express' left Manchester Piccadilly station at 10.30am and was booked to arrive at Bournemouth West at 5.32pm. On Saturdays it had a much easier schedule, despite having no advertised stops between Stockport and Cheltenham. *Colour-Rail*

The operational problems of summer Saturday working on the S&D are evidenced here as LMSR Class 2P 4-4-0 No.40700, paired with BR Standard Class 5MT No.73051, is held at Midford's up outer home signal with the 9.55am Bournemouth West to Leeds, whilst Class 4F No.44523 piloting S&D 2-8-0 No.53801 clears the single line section from Bath. The line from here to Wellow followed the course of an old plateway constructed at the end of the eighteenth century to carry coal from the mines around Radstock to the canal at Midford. The tramway kept closely to the sides of the valleys and consequently the line was characterised on this stretch by constant reverse curves and abrupt changes of gradient. On some stretches, however, some of the plateway's twists and turns were too tight for even the S&D to follow. This picture is thought to date from the summer of 1959. *R. C. Riley*

A classic view of Wellow, showing the up 'Pines Express' heading northwards on 25th August 1962: the train engine is BR Standard Class 9F 2-10-0 No.92001, with BR Standard Class 4MT No.75009 as pilot locomotive. The tower of St. Julian's church can be seen on the right above the trees. The S&D line is famous for the amazing combinations of motive power that could be observed but in this picture the variety of the carriages forming the train is worthy of note. The first coach is a LMSR-designed BSK (brake second corridor) which appears to be newly repainted, whilst the second vehicle – a most unusual sight on the S&D – is a stray BR Standard carriage in chocolate and cream livery which would almost certainly have been allocated to one of the Western Region's named express sets! The third vehicle is a Gresley-designed teak bodied carriage, so the first three coaches really are a bit of an assortment. The remainder of the train is comprised mainly of BR Standard vehicles in maroon livery. *Roy Hobbs*

A portrait of the beautifully maintained station at Wellow (6¾ miles from Bath) which nestled in an idyllic, secluded steeply-sided valley. This picture was taken on 6th July 1959, a lovely summer's day. The main station building, built of grey limestone, was of a modest size and consisted of the stationmaster's office, combined booking office and waiting room and a ladies' room. There was also a stone-built store room and shed used as a lamp room. The down platform had only a wooden shelter to protect passengers from the elements. The goods yard was still open at the time of this picture but closed in June 1963. The village of Wellow was poorly served by buses due to it being surrounded by very steep hills and consequently the station was well patronised by local people, who were hit very hard when the line was closed. *R. C. Riley*

The station running-in board at Shoscombe & Single Hill Halt was obviously built to last! This shot was taken on 11th December 1965. *Michael Allen*

Shoscombe & Single Hill Halt (8½ miles from Bath) was opened on 23rd September 1929, at a time when the railways were starting to feel the effects of competition from road transport, especially in the movement of milk traffic. In addition, passenger receipts were being affected by the growth of rural bus services. The halt was constructed of standard Southern Railway concrete and steel components and was a very basic affair without any buildings on the platforms. There was, however, a small booking office and waiting room on the pathway leading up to the village. This station may not have been the most impressive on the S&D, but at least it fulfilled a useful role because, like at Wellow, local roads were very steep. This picture was also taken on 11th December 1965, looking towards Bath. *Michael Allen*

A scene at Writhlington, showing a very dirty BR Standard Class 5MT, No.73092, shunting a goods train on 31st October 1964. Writhlington marked the boundary between the pastoral countryside of northern Somerset and the start of the North Somerset coalfield with its associated pit winding gear and slag heaps which seemed totally alien in this otherwise unspoilt part of the world. Latterly, there were two collieries in this immediate area, Lower Writhlington and Braysdown, the former being established as long ago as 1829. It survived to become the final working mine in the coalfield, lasting until 28th September 1973. The small settlement at Writhlington did not justify a passenger station but there was a signal box that controlled entry to the sidings which led to the mines. The last section of track on the original S&D route to be removed was taken up here in the mid-1970s. *Michael Chown*

The North Somerset coalfield was largely centred on Radstock and in times gone by there were three collieries in the town's immediate environs, Ludlow's, Middle Pit and Tyning. In addition to the 'main lines' that served Radstock there was also a network of narrow gauge tramways but all of these had apparently been converted to standard gauge before the First World War. There was a small engine shed at Radstock – a sub shed of Bath (Green Park) – where locomotives employed on local shunting duties were stabled and in this view a pair of LMSR Class 3F 0-6-0Ts, which were universally known as 'Jinties', pose outside the depot in May 1960. Note the pit waste tips in the background. The main S&D running lines were the tracks farthest from the camera and passed just in front of the stone wall. *Alan Jarvis*

The 3.20pm Bath to Bournemouth West train, hauled by BR Standard Class 4MT 4-6-0 No.75073, enters Radstock North station on 26th June 1965. No.75073 was a product of Swindon Works, entering traffic in November 1955. It was among the first locomotives of its class transferred to Bath shed in 1956, the others being sister engines Nos.75071/2. No.75073 lasted in service until December 1965. The large building on the right at the end of the goods yard is the engine shed. When the first of the S&D Class 7F 2-8-0s entered service they were not permitted to use Bath shed and were based instead at Radstock. Following closure of the S&D line to passenger services the shed at Radstock was retained to stable a Class 08 diesel shunter and did not finally close for BR purposes until 19th November 1973, by which time it was administered by Westbury depot. It was leased by a preservation group until November 1975 and the building was eventually demolished in 1980, when yet another tangible link with the past disappeared forever. Note the solidly-built stone cottages on the left of the picture which are a familiar feature in this part of Somerset.
Roy Patterson

Opposite lower: Some of the sidings at Radstock could only be reached after passing under Tyning's Bridge – known to S&D enginemen as the 'Marble Arch' – which had a very restricted clearance of only 10ft 10in from rail level to the roof of the arch. Consequently only the smallest locomotives could be used and for some time these workings were the preserve of three small 0-4-0STs (known locally as the 'Dazzlers') that had been constructed at Highbridge Works. These were replaced in 1929 by a pair of geared Sentinel shunters of unorthodox appearance which, in BR days, were numbered 47190 and 47191. The latter machine was withdrawn in August 1959 but its sister engine survived until March 1961 and this is depicted outside Radstock shed, also in May 1960. When one of the Sentinels was temporarily transferred away in the late 1940s, BR appear to have scoured the country to secure a replacement and this resulted in diminutive Lancashire & Yorkshire Railway Class 0F 'Pug' 0-4-0ST No.51202 visiting Radstock. *Alan Jarvis*

Another BR Standard Class 5MT 4-6-0 on a freight working. Radstock station is depicted showing an up empty coal train from Norton Hill colliery running through behind No.73001 on a misty 3rd April 1965. The photographer comments that this engine was a recent transfer to Bath (Green Park) shed and stood out from other locomotives of its class due to its chime whistle! In BR days the premises here were known as Radstock North presumably to distinguish it from the adjacent former GWR Radstock West station, on the Bristol to Frome line. *Hugh Ballantyne*

A general view of Radstock station (10³/₄ miles from Bath) recorded on 18th August 1962. Note the neat and tidy appearance of the station and attractive flower beds. The signal box visible is Radstock North B box (formerly known as Radstock West) and this guarded the level crossing over the busy A367 Bath to Shepton Mallet road. This crossing, together with that over the GWR line, caused lengthy hold-ups to road users and must have been the source of many caustic comments by motorists over the years. The crossing gates at Radstock must also have given rise to similar expressions by enginemen of down trains, because they marked the start of the long climb – much of it on a gradient of 1 in 50 – to Masbury summit, and the crew knew that much hard work lay ahead. *Michael Allen*

The climb of the Mendip hills began (as previously mentioned) immediately Radstock station had been passed, the line rising at a gradient of 1 in 50 from the platform end. In this picture S&D Class 7F 2-8-0 No.53808 is seen tackling the ascent with the 2.00pm Bath to Templecombe goods train on 12th September 1962. Fortunately for the enginemen the train is conveying quite a modest load so the locomotive would not have been unduly taxed. In less than half a mile the S&D line had gained sufficient height to enable it to cross above the former GWR Bristol to Frome line.
John Beckett

Between Radstock and Midsomer Norton the S&D route climbs through a cleft in the hills which separates the towns and here the 9.08am Birmingham New Street to Bournemouth West train is seen heading upgrade on 18th August 1962. The line is rising at an unrelenting 1 in 50 at this point. The locomotives in charge are S&D Class 7F 2-8-0 No.53809 piloted by BR Standard Class 5MT 4-6-0 No.73049, which were probably making fairly light work of the modest eight-coach load. Another picture of this train, passing Moorewood, appears elsewhere in this album. *Michael Allen*

In late 1963 Bournemouth shed decided to try out a BR Standard Class 4MT 2-6-4T locomotive on the 1.10pm Bournemouth to Bath and 7.05pm return which were rostered for a Southern Region locomotive. The first recorded appearance of one of these engines on the S&D was on 4th November 1963. These machines quickly proved to be successful and competent performers, being ideally suited to the modest three and four coach trains then being operated. Here, No.80096 is depicted making a spirited ascent of the 1 in 50 incline between Radstock and Midsomer Norton with the 4.20pm Bath to Bournemouth train on an almost cloudless 26th June 1965. Like most of these versatile engines, No.80096 was built at Brighton Works, in this particular case in November 1954, and it lasted until December 1965. *Roy Patterson*

Holiday-makers travelling down from the industrial north of England must have been shocked when their train passed through the North Somerset coalfield which had a similar environment to some parts of the north, albeit on a smaller scale. In this portrait of a grim industrial scene more associated with the mining districts of County Durham or Yorkshire, BR Standard Class 4MT No.75072, hauling the 3.20pm Bath to Templecombe train, passes Norton Hill colliery slag heap near Midsomer Norton on 1st July 1961. Some time before this picture was taken the late running down 'Pines Express' had passed through behind LMSR Class 2P 4-4-0 No.40634 piloting Bulleid Pacific No.34047 *Callington* and sparks from the engines had set areas of vegetation alight, this being tinder dry after a long drought. The resulting conflagration required the attendance of the local fire brigade who extinguished the flames before any real damage was done. The first shaft was sunk at Norton Hill in 1839 and the mine eventually became the most productive in the coalfield with more than 149,000 tons being extracted in 1949, this activity bringing much valuable traffic to the S&D line. New sidings were laid in 1953 and the pit underwent extensive modernisation in the early 1960s. Despite this investment the colliery was closed on 11th February 1966, shortly before the railway. The mine had its own steam shunting locomotive and latterly this was an 0-6-0ST, *Lord Salisbury,* which had been built by Pecketts of Bristol in 1906. *R.C.Riley*

A loaded coal train gingerly descends from Norton Hill colliery to Midsomer Norton station behind LMSR 'Jinty' 0-6-0T No.47544 on 1st September 1965. The S&D 'main line' tracks are visible immediately behind the locomotive, while beyond lies the townscape of Midsomer Norton. Bearing testament to the town's industrial heritage, note in the middle distance the slag heap which had completely grassed over by the time of this picture. *Roger Merry-Price*

The train featured in the previous picture is seen again and the apparent identity of the 'driver' is revealed: a young lad looks out from the cab of the 'Jinty'! Perhaps he was the son of one of the enginemen or a local schoolboy who simply wanted to experience the thrill of a short footplate ride – who knows? An unidentified Stanier Class 8F 2-8-0, coupled on the other end of the train, later took the load down to Bath. The single track from the colliery can be clearly made out on the right in the middle distance whilst the main line descends at 1 in 50 on the left of the shot. *Charles Whetmath*

A loaded coal train sets off from Midsomer Norton towards Bath on 3rd July 1961. The train engine is S&D Class 7F 2-8-0 No.53810 with LMSR 'Jinty' No.47316 as pilot, running bunker first. It is likely that the 'Jinty' had been carrying out shunting duties at Norton Hill colliery and was merely returning to Radstock on the front of the train to save a 'light engine' movement. A porter is almost lost in the shadow on the right of the shot: he appears to be dealing with pigeon baskets. The S&D saw heavy pigeon traffic and often special trains, invariably hauled by S&D Class 7Fs, were run to convey this traffic. *R. C. Riley*

The station at Midsomer Norton (12½ miles from Bath) was inconveniently situated at the top of a hill to the south of the town, but the station staff would no doubt have argued that the journey was worth the effort just to see their beautifully kept station which was one of the best maintained on the S&D route. Neat and colourful flower beds, hanging baskets and perfectly trimmed lawns: it was no wonder that Midsomer Norton won the 'best kept station' award year after year. Prizes for the most attractive station flower display had been given since the S&D Joint Committee initiated the scheme way back in 1913 and, almost needless to say, Midsomer Norton had been one of the very first prizewinners. *Michael Allen*

RADSTOCK TO MIDSOMER NORTON

After the end of the Second World War holidays with pay became the norm for the masses, but the era of cheap continental trips had not yet arrived and the average British family took their annual holiday at the seaside. The date of the exodus was largely dictated by the school summer holidays in July and August and this put an enormous strain on the railway's resources, especially on the S&D line where the heavier trains had to be piloted over the Mendip hills' fierce gradients. Movements were also constrained by three separate sections of single line which were undoubtedly bottlenecks when traffic was heavy. It could be argued that the S&D reached its zenith in the 1950s when there was a never-ending procession of weekend 'dated' holiday extras, including overnight trains, and every locomotive that could turn a wheel was pressed into service. These next three pictures that follow were all taken on 25th June 1955 and, hopefully, convey something of the flavour of the S&D line during this period. Here, the fireman of LMSR Class 2P 4-4-0 No.40568 is seen taking a breather as his engine assists BR Standard Class 5MT 4-6-0 No.73074 on the long, hard ascent from Midsomer Norton to Chilcompton tunnel. *Trevor Owen*

In the 1950s a number of Stanier 'Black Fives' were allocated to Bath (Green Park) shed and in May 1951 Nos. 44826/30/39, 44917 and 45440 were officially based there. The last of these locomotives was moved away from Bath in 1958 when replaced by BR Standard Class 5MT 4-6-0s and it is therefore not surprising that action photographs of 'Black Fives' working on the S&D line proved particularly elusive, so the author was delighted when this shot was submitted for publication. In this illustration No.45440, piloted by Class 4F No.44417, is also seen at grips with the steep climb up to Chilcompton tunnel. No.45440 later spent some years based at Edge Hill shed, Liverpool, a far cry indeed from Somerset, and was withdrawn from there in September 1967. *Trevor Owen*

Photographed on 25th June 1955, the same day as the previous two pictures, LMSR Class 4F 0-6-0 No.44557 is about to plunge into the gloom of Chilcompton tunnel with a southbound local train. The line followed the lie of the land as far as practicable but a bluff in the hillside at this point necessitated a tunnel: it was only 66 yards long so the locomotive crew's period of discomfort would have been brief. The tunnel had separate bores for each track, this being a reminder that the S&D was originally constructed as a single line. Doubling of most of the northern section of line took place in the 1880s, the stretch from Radstock to Binegar being completed in 1886. *Trevor Owen*

One can only imagine the ear-shattering sound being emitted by LMSR Class 8F 2-8-0 No.48706 as it leaves Chilcompton tunnel and attacks the 1 in 53 climb towards Masbury summit. The Class 8F was powering the Great Western Society's farewell special on 5th March 1966 which ran from Bath to Bournemouth and back. Note the safety vales are lifting slightly, indicating that the fireman was doing a good job. *Trevor Owen*

The S&D Class 7F 2-8-0s were constructed specifically to work goods trains over the line and virtually monopolised this traffic since their introduction. By the late 1950s, however, these locomotives were starting to show their age and the first example was withdrawn in July 1959. On 3rd May 1961 LMSR Class 8F 2-8-0 No.48450 was tested over the route in order to assess the class's suitability as replacements for the 7Fs. The trial run was a great success and Nos.48436 and 48471 were allocated to Green Park shed. The S&D 7Fs were gradually reduced in numbers over the ensuing few years, with engines presumably being taken out of use as they became due for heavy overhaul. The reduction in the number of Class 7Fs was matched by a corresponding increase in LMSR Class 8Fs and in this picture No.48660 is seen leaving Chilcompton tunnel with the 11.15am Bath to Templecombe freight train on 17th August 1962. The Western Region was actively running down the S&D route at this time and one manifestation of this was the dwindling amount of freight traffic being carried, as evidenced here by No.48660's pitiful load. Pictures of these engines on freight duty have proved extremely elusive, the reason being that most enthusiasts visited the line at weekends when goods trains were not running. By December 1964 six Class 8Fs were officially allocated to Bath (Green Park) shed, these being Nos. 48309, 48409/44, 48525, 48660 and 48737 and engines of this class remained there until the bitter end in March 1966. *Colour-Rail*

Many pictures have been taken over the years of trains climbing out of Chilcompton tunnel but here, for a change, is a shot of an up train descending towards the tunnel. The locomotives depicted are LMSR Class 2P 4-4-0 No.40697 and (what appears to be) Bulleid 'West Country' Class Pacific No.34043 *Combe Martin* heading towards Bath with an unidentified express in August 1961. The village of Chilcompton forms the backdrop to the photograph. Note how the line climbs steeply towards Chilcompton station which is out of sight farther around the curve. The S&D was certainly not a route for poorly steaming engines or faint-hearted enginemen! *Roy Hobbs*

Photographed on a misty autumn morning, BR Standard Class 5MT 4-6-0 No.73054 exerts maximum effort as it climbs the 1 in 50 up to Chilcompton station with the 9.53am Bath to Bournemouth semi-fast train on 31st October 1964. This train actually started at Bristol, so is perhaps more accurately described as a Bristol to Bournemouth working. It left there at 9.03am and arrived at Bournemouth West at 1.02pm; this journey time included a wait of twenty-two minutes at Templecombe, so it was hardly a speedy trip. *Alan Reeve*

Surely, one of the most memorable sights during the twilight years of Southern steam was that of two immaculately turned-out unmodified Bulleid Pacifics, Nos.34006 *Bude* and 34057 *Biggin Hill*, hauling the LCGB rail tour in glorious early spring sunshine on the penultimate day of the S&D line. What a pity it was such a desperately sad occasion! Here the pair glint in the late afternoon sun as they attack the climb towards Chilcompton. *Charles Whetmath*

Facing page The fireman of the 10.32am Bournemouth West to Manchester Piccadilly gives the photographer a friendly wave as his train passes Moorewood sidings, between Binegar and Chilcompton, on 18th August 1962. Motive power is BR Standard Class 9F 2-10-0 No.92001. Note the two rather fine vintage lower quadrant signals which were presumably worked from the nineteen-lever Moorewood signal box, the last to be opened on the line, that is visible behind the rear coach of the train. This used to be a fascinating spot for industrial archaeologists, as well as railway enthusiasts, because a nearby quarry was connected to the sidings in the foreground by an aerial ropeway. In addition, a two-foot gauge tramway ran from Moorewood colliery to the sidings, but both of these operations had ceased by 1930. Latterly, the sidings owed their retention to the fact that they were used for wagon storage. A further installation of interest is Emborough stone works, of which some of the buildings can just be discerned hidden in the trees some distance behind the signal box. After being operated on a single shift only basis for some time, the signal box finally closed on 21st June 1965. *Colour-Rail*

Above Another picture taken at Moorewood on the same date, this time looking towards Chilcompton, with the 9.08am Birmingham to Bournemouth train passing in charge of S&D Class 7F 2-8-0 No.53809 piloted by BR Standard Class 5MT No.73049. The bridge carried an unclassified road from Emborough to Downside across the railway. The 1 in 50/1 in 53 gradients which had applied all of the way from Radstock moderated slightly at Moorewood to 1 in 66 and there were even three brief stretches of level track in the vicinity, which provided short respites for engine crews. From Moorewood to the summit the average gradient was 1 in 70 or thereabouts. The people standing by the tent wave to the passing train, whilst the photographer was no doubt grateful to obtain a photograph of such an interesting combination of locomotives which, of course, could not be found on any other line in the country. *Colour-Rail*

The 7.45am Bradford Forster Square to Bournemouth train, headed by BR Standard Class 9F 2-10-0 No.92233, passes Binegar's down distant signal, also on 18th August 1962. The Southern Railway never used to waste anything and the signal, one of many others across the system, had been fashioned from two old sections of rail bolted together. In contrast Moorewood's up distant signal has a lower quadrant arm and a London & South Western Railway lattice post. One or two of the passengers are leaning out of windows, perhaps to get a better view of the scenery or maybe to obtain a little bit of fresh air on a hot day. They were probably hoping for many more during their holiday by the seaside! *Michael Allen*

One of the author's favourite S&D photographs – for more than one reason! This picture was taken at the same location as the previous shot, but from the other side of the line and, most importantly, in beautifully soft autumn sunshine. It shows S&D 2-8-0 No.53809 heaving a down goods train uphill towards Binegar with LMSR 'Jinty' No.47496 pushing for all it is worth at the rear – a true masterpiece. This portrait was taken on 6th October 1962. One of the principal problems during the compilation of this album was the dearth of shots of S&D 2-8-0s working goods trains. These engines were designed for goods work over the line but were not widely photographed in colour performing this role because comparatively few photographers visited the S&D line on Mondays to Fridays. In contrast, pictures of these locomotives on Saturday seasonal passenger duty are plentiful but hardly representative of the yeoman service they gave the S&D line over the years. *R. C. Riley*

Binegar station's up-side waiting shelter and signal box are seen in this picture taken on 11th December 1965. In 1956 BR produced an instructional film on emergency single line working and, because no trains operated on Sundays between Bath and Evercreech Junction after the end of the summer timetable, it was decided that this would be an ideal location. The filming took place on Sundays in late September and October largely between Shepton Mallet and Binegar, which had their names changed to 'Averton Hammer' and 'Boiland' respectively so that the film, which was for general distribution throughout the system, would not be associated with any particular area. BR Standard locomotives, which were commonplace throughout the country, were used for the passenger workings, but on the third Sunday a highly distinctive S&D Class 7F 2-8-0, carrying the goods headlamp code that was peculiar to the S&D, was turned out for the goods train scenes which rather let the cat out of the bag! *Michael Allen*

The station at Binegar (17 miles from Bath) served only a small village and had very modest facilities, the main building being on the down side. It is seen in this picture which was also taken on 11th December 1965. The poster on the wall concerns the closure of Bournemouth West station which was shut from 6th September 1965. Pilot locomotives were sometimes detached from northbound trains here but one of the most interesting aspects of operation concerned down goods trains, which were often banked from Radstock to Masbury summit. The banking engine collected a 'banking engine staff' from the tablet exchange apparatus at Binegar that permitted the engine to run back 'wrong line' from the summit to Binegar. There was special equipment in Binegar signal box that provided the necessary interlocking security to enable the 'wrong direction' movement to be undertaken safely. Like at nearby Moorewood, in times gone by there were some interesting installations at Binegar. In 1904 a two miles-long three-foot gauge tramway was laid by the Oakhill Brewery to connect their establishment with the main line. Two 0-4-0T locomotives, *Oakhill* and *Mendip,* worked this line until it closed in 1921. Between Moorewood and Binegar a siding serving the Mendips stone works trailed in on the down side. Stone was carried from the quarries by an aerial ropeway. *Michael Allen*

The S&D line was renowned for its remarkable locomotive combinations – where else could one see a Bulleid 'West Country' Class Pacific being assisted by an LMSR 4F Class 0-6-0? The locomotives concerned are Nos.34043 *Combe Martin* and 44102, and note that the Bulleid engine is carrying the 'Pines Express' headboard. The location is the Oakhill road bridge, less than a quarter of a mile from Masbury summit, and the date is 18th August 1962. *Michael Allen*

The same location is seen again from a new viewpoint and in totally different lighting conditions. The train is a heavy down freight, headed by S&D 2-8-0 No.53809, which is seen in an earlier picture near Binegar, and some quick motoring enabled the photographer to obtain a further photograph of the train approaching Masbury summit with 'Jinty' No.47496 still pushing mightily at the rear. After 7½ miles of almost continuous climbing the summit is nearly in sight and the 7F's crew could take it relatively easy as their train continued downhill towards Evercreech Junction. The 'Jinty', as previously mentioned, would have returned 'wrong line' to Binegar before setting off for its base at Radstock. *R.C. Riley*

The summit at last! BR Standard Class 5MT 4-6-0 No.73051 has just passed under the road bridge (from where the previous picture was taken) and breasts Masbury summit with a down van train, almost certainly a pigeon special, on 18th August 1962. The train appears to be formed of LMSR-designed full brake vehicles (known to railwaymen as BGs) which were entirely open inside apart from a central guard's compartment. Two sets of double doors on each side of the vehicle provided ample access for the loading of parcels and suchlike: there was also a single central guard's door on each side. *Colour-Rail*

Another picture taken at Masbury summit, 811 feet above sea level, this time looking southwards. The up 'Pines Express' powered by BR Standard Class 4MT 4-6-0 No.75009 piloting Class 9F 2-10-0 No.92245, is seen surmounting the summit, also on 18th August 1962. Trains approaching the summit from the north had to contend with a relatively easy 1 in 73 gradient for the final stage of the climb but trains coming up from the south faced the more daunting challenge of about three miles at 1 in 50, a much tougher proposition. The climb to Masbury was difficult enough in favourable weather conditions, but on a drizzly day the rail conditions could become very slippery and enginemen had to call upon all their skill and experience to avoid a locomotive slipping to a stand. *Colour-Rail*

LMSR-designed Class 4F 0-6-0 No.44422 assists BR Standard Class 5MT 4-6-0 No.73050 over Masbury summit with the 10.05am Bournemouth West to Derby train on 9th July 1960. Judging by the locomotives' exhausts, both machines were being worked 'flat out', but the really hard work was over for the crews once the summit had been passed and they could relax to some degree as their train sped downhill towards Radstock. Both of these locomotives subsequently survived into preservation. *R. C. Riley*

A panoramic view of Masbury Halt (18¾ miles from Bath) looking north: this picture was taken on 12th July 1960. The station served a few scattered communities and was probably never well used, this no doubt being a factor in the decision to downgrade it to a halt in 1935 and remove all staff (apart from the signalman) from 26th September 1938. The station buildings here were concentrated on the up platform, the down platform only being provided with a simple waiting shelter. The stone-built structure furthest from the camera housed the waiting rooms and booking office, whilst the twenty-lever signal box, which was closed from 1st July 1964, occupies a prominent position in the centre of the platform. The building nearest to the camera is the stationmaster's house, a solid-looking, stone-built structure with a bay window which boasted an eye-catching stone carving of an imaginary mediaeval castle and the Gothic legend 'Maesbury Castle'. After the First World War church services were held in the waiting room on Sunday evenings, this presumably being the most suitable venue in the immediate vicinity. There was a small goods yard on the up side but this was closed from 10th June 1963. The course of an old siding will be noted on the right of the picture, this being the headshunt for a siding that served a stone crushing plant prior to the Second World War. This installation was apparently demolished in the late 1930s and the sidings extended to serve a United States army base. *R.C. Riley*

In a photograph full of interest, the double-headed 2.00pm Templecombe to Bath train, hauled by BR Standard Class 4MT 2-6-4T No.80138 with bunker-first Ivatt Class 2MT 2-6-2T No.41307 as pilot, has emerged from Winsor Hill tunnel and passes the long-disused Ham Wood quarry sidings on 5th March 1966. Note the coat of arms being carried on the bunker of the leading locomotive. It should be noted that there were two separate single line tunnels here, the portal visible in the distance was the down line tunnel entrance, the up line tunnel's northern portal being out of sight around the bend. There was an incline here which used to link the quarry to the sidings in the foreground and adjacent stone crushing plant. In addition, Winsor Hill quarry, dating from 1875, was located on the down side of the line and this was also served by a siding: part of the quarry face is just visible above the leading locomotive. The shell of Winsor Hill signal box can be seen towards the rear of the train. This was the only box on the line to be constructed entirely of stone and stood derelict for many years following its closure in August 1948. *Trevor Owen*

Spectators line the trackside as the Locomotive Club of Great Britain's 'Somerset & Dorset' tour heads towards Bath on 5th March 1966, the final day of normal operations on the route. By the date of this photograph the last Class 4F 0-6-0s and S&D 2-8-0s on the line had been withdrawn for some time, so a pair of Bulleid Pacifics was selected to haul the train from Evercreech Junction to Bath and back to Templecombe. Here Nos.34006 *Bude* and 34057 *Biggin Hill* approach Winsor Hill tunnel and the two powerful Bulleids were no doubt ascending the 1 in 50 incline at this point with consummate ease. It will be noted that the up line takes a different course to the down line. The route from Evercreech to Bath was originally single track and when doubling occurred on this section in 1892 the contractor realised that considerable expenditure on tunnelling could be saved by deviating a short distance westwards. The original tunnel, which became the down line, was 242 yards long whereas the new tunnel was only 132 yards long. The down line is out of sight in the cutting on the left of the shot. *Charles Whetmath*

For a change, a photograph taken from a train (albeit a rail tour) which gives, hopefully, some idea of the S&D as seen from the passenger's viewpoint. The white exhaust steam being emitted by Nos.53807 and 44558 stands out against a dark sky as they toil upgrade towards Masbury summit with the Home Counties Railway Society 'Somerset & Dorset' tour on 7th June 1964. The S&D was noted for the pride and dedication of its staff – note the neat edge to the track ballast. *Michael Chown*

The death throes of the Somerset & Dorset. The 2.00pm Templecombe to Bath train (which is depicted in a previous illustration) crosses Charlton Road viaduct, Shepton Mallet, on 5th March 1966. This was the final day of ordinary services and in order to simplify disposal arrangements No.41307 was being worked northwards to Bath where most of the remaining S&D steam locomotives were congregated. The massive twenty-seven arch, 317 yards-long viaduct, which carried the railway across part of the town, is undoubtedly the most impressive civil engineering structure on the line and the short train looks somewhat insignificant. Remarkably, there is a change of gradient on the viaduct. Trains leaving Shepton Mallet in a northerly direction are on a falling gradient of 1 in 55 but halfway across the gradient changes to 1 in 66 against up trains, which later steepens to 1 in 50. This is most unlikely to have troubled the crews on this working, however, the two locomotives being more than adequate power for the featherweight load of just three coaches. *Michael Chown*

Shepton Mallet (Charlton Road) station (21¾ miles from Bath) on 18th August 1962 with the 4.15pm Templecombe to Bath stopping train running into the platform behind LMSR Class 4F 0-6-0 No.44417. The suffix 'Charlton Road' was used in order to avoid confusion with the former GWR High Street station on the Yatton to Witham line. The coaches forming the train are an LMSR 3-set, so the entire train is of LMSR origin! The principal station buildings here were on the up platform, whilst the twenty-six lever signal box plus a small waiting room were on the down platform. There was a fair-sized layout at Shepton Mallet, the goods yard (closed from 10th June 1963) being on the up side south of the station, while in times past a stone crushing plant was on the opposite side of the line north of the station. The signal inspector for the entire line had his office and a small workshop at Shepton Mallet. *Michael Allen*

On 8th July 1960 BBC Television descended on the S&D line to do some filming for the 'Railway Roundabout' programme. It was arranged that they would film the 11.00am goods train from Bath to Evercreech Junction and S&D Class 7F 2-8-0 No.53807 was specially spruced up for the occasion. Here No.53807, in uncharacteristically sparkling condition for a Bath (Green Park) engine, is seen taking water at Shepton Mallet. Most unusually, at the request of the BBC production team, the train was banked up to Combe Down tunnel by sister engine No.53801 but this machine had not been cleaned and was in the usual grubby condition. These sturdy locomotives were designed at Derby specially for use on the S&D and built in two batches, Nos.53800 to 53805 at Derby in 1914 and the remainder by Robert Stephenson & Hawthorns at Darlington in 1925. Built primarily for freight haulage, the Class 7Fs were latterly often pressed into passenger traffic on summer Saturdays, a favourite turn being the Cleethorpes to Exmouth train in both directions. These engines, which were remarkably sure-footed and rarely known to slip when in the hands of a competent driver, were able to take ten coaches over the Mendips, two more than the maximum unassisted load for a Standard Class 5MT or a Bulleid Pacific. Withdrawals commenced in 1959 and by early 1962 all of the 1914-built series had gone for scrap. The last survivor was No.53807, this engine being withdrawn in September 1964 – the end of an era at Green Park depot! *Colour-Rail*

Another scene at Shepton Mallet station, this time showing S&D Class 7F 2-8-0 No.53805, in charge of the 12.35pm down freight from Bath, 'blowing off' as it takes water at the southern end of the station on 26th September 1959. Part of the signal box is visible above the train. Judging by the overcast conditions the photographer appears to have been very fortunate to obtain a picture with the sun shining. Note the intricate trackwork, this being a neglected facet of railway engineering that has never caught the imagination of many people. Nowadays track components are standardised as much as possible to save money, thus robbing much interest from this aspect of railways. *R.C. Riley*

Apparently photographed from the signal box, the 9.25am Bournemouth to Liverpool and Manchester train approaches Shepton Mallet station on 1st September 1962 behind BR Standard Class 5MT No.73047 with S&D Class 7F 2-8-0 No.53808 as pilot. It was quite unusual to see one of these 2-8-0s used as a pilot locomotive. This train was booked to stop only at Poole, Blandford Forum and Evercreech Junction and was due into Bath (Green Park) at 11.45am. In the background the bridge that carried the former GWR Yatton to Witham line over the S&D route can just be discerned. The original bridge was a brick arch while the later bridge, installed when the route was doubled in 1892, was of the girder type. *R.C. Riley*

The eleven-arch Prestleigh viaduct was an extremely graceful structure which seemed to blend excellently with the surrounding Somerset hills: what a shame the area had been disfigured by intrusive and unsightly pylons. Here, LMSR Class 8F 2-8-0 No.48309, a Crewe Works product dating from 1943, 'blows off' as it sweeps downhill with the LCGB's 'Wessex Downsman' rail tour on 4th April 1965, a pleasant spring day. The train is formed of a uniform set of green coaches and its appearance is enhanced by prominent roofboards. This locomotive was one of only two members of its class equipped with steam heating. This apparatus was fitted in 1955 when No.48309 worked the Royal Train in connection with HM the Queen's visit to Wales. *Roy Hobbs*

In this everyday scene, S&D Class 7F 2-8-0 No.53809 is illustrated pausing between shunting duties just north of Evercreech Junction station on 6th July 1959. The track immediately to the right of the camera position is the single line to Highbridge, while the track on the left served as a shunting neck for the yard. Note the profusion of four-wheeled wooden-bodied wagons, designs that have long since been eliminated from the national railway system. On the right is a cattle wagon, of which there were thousands in use in times gone by – those were the days! *R. C. Riley*

An up empty coaching stock train is seen at Evercreech Junction on 5th July 1959 behind Bulleid 'West Country' Pacific No.34044 *Woolacombe*. Bulleid Pacifics were first allocated to Bath (Green Park) in the early 1950s and in May 1951 Nos.34040 to 34044 were officially based at that shed which was then under Southern Region jurisdiction. Locomotives of this class had a tendency to slip, however, and this, together with their enormous appetite for coal, ensured that their stay was short. Bulleid engines continued to work regularly on the S&D line from the Bournemouth end for many years thereafter but their appearances were reduced considerably following the withdrawal of through inter-regional services in September 1962. *R. C. Riley*

Portrait of a loyal workhorse. On 30th September 1962 the LCGB sponsored the 'Somerset & Dorset' rail tour, one of the highlights being haulage over the Mendip hills by a S&D Class 7F 2-8-0. No.53808 was assigned to this duty and in this illustration it is seen 'blowing off' in the goods yard at Evercreech Junction while awaiting the return of the train from Burnham-on-Sea. How much nicer these machines looked after a spot of cleaning! *Rodney Lissenden*

In the early 1960s the sight of LMSR Class 2P 4-4-0s standing on the middle siding at Evercreech Junction before attaching themselves to the front of a northbound express was an everyday occurrence, so 'everyday' in fact that very few people apparently bothered to photograph it in colour. In this shot an up train has just departed as a BR Standard Class 5MT comes cautiously down the bank into the station. On the left an unidentified Class 2P raises steam in the middle siding, its fireman no doubt mindful of the stern task that lies ahead. After forty year's sterling service the Class 2Ps were ousted from piloting duties at the end of the 1961 summer timetable, the final survivor on the S&D being No.40537 which managed to escape withdrawal until September 1962. *Alan Jarvis*

The dying days of the S&D. In this typical scene from the last months of operation, very grimy BR Standard Class 4MT 4-6-0 No.75072 starts away from Evercreech Junction and begins the long climb to Masbury summit watched by a substantial crowd of onlookers. This picture was taken on 6th November 1965. *Michael Allen*

GWR 2251 Class 0-6-0 No.3210 stands in the down platform at Evercreech Junction station (26½ miles from Bath) on 2nd June 1962 after arrival with a train from Highbridge. The premises here were known simply as 'Evercreech' until the extension to Bath opened on 20th July 1874 and the station gained junction status. Another train occupies the up platform. Part of the main station buildings, including the stationmaster's house, are visible on the right: note the flower beds and (what appear to be) climbing rose bushes. The small down side goods yard, which is out of sight on the right, consisted of a goods shed, two cranes and cattle pens. *Roy Denison*

Opposite: Class 7F 2-8-0 No.53807 and Class 4F 0-6-0 No.44558 shunt across the main road at the south end of Evercreech Junction station during the course of working a Home Counties Railway Society rail tour on 7th June 1964. Note that both locomotives' cabs appear to be crowded with enthusiasts having a footplate ride and there are also one or two people wandering about near the running lines. In those days there was a much more relaxed official attitude towards such behaviour. This is thought to have been the last time two former S&D locomotives worked together – a very sad occasion. The two engines had worked down to Bournemouth the previous day initially on the 8.15am Bath to Templecombe, and later continuing from Templecombe to Bournemouth 'light engines'. No.53807 lasted a further three months in service while No.44558 soldiered on until December 1964. The latter was one of five of these engines built for the S&D by Armstrong Whitworth & Co. in 1922 and they were universally known to enginemen as 'Armstrongs'. *Michael Chown*

SHEPTON MALLET TO EVERCREECH JUNCTION

HCRS

HOME COUNTIES
RAILWAY SOCIETY

S.&D. RLY TOUR

53807

82

A genuine S&D car parking sign! This relic survived at Evercreech Junction until the end but was apparently stolen on the last day. *John Beckett*

The management of the old Somerset & Dorset Railway obviously took their responsibility to guard against fire very seriously, and rightly so. This picture was taken at Evercreech Junction on 26th March 1964. *Michael Chown*

Far left: A rather fine signalling specimen at Evercreech Junction. This lower quadrant bracket signal was positioned at the north end of the yard; the ringed signal controlled entry to the goods line which runs behind the signal box. *Roy Denison*

Left: A wreath and black ribbons adorn a closure notice at Evercreech Junction on 5th March 1966. In just a few words a BR poster coldly announces the official death sentence on the S&D line which was held in such great affection by so many people. After years of deliberately starving the line of traffic and making no effort to introduce more economical working or attract passengers the Western Region had finally got its way, and this at a time when there was supposedly a moratorium on further railway closures while a newly-elected government reviewed transport policy. *Alan Chandler*

A view of the layout at Evercreech Junction on 30th March 1964. The Highbridge branch goes straight ahead whilst the line to Bath curves very sharply to the right: the North signal box is on the left. The peculiar signal is an S&D backing signal which was used here during shunting operations. It authorised the driver of a goods train that had arrived from Bath to reverse on the down main line and set back along the branch and into the up goods yard. *Michael Chown*

Photographed on 6th July 1959, an almost cloudless summer's day, the fireman of the 2.20pm Highbridge to Evercreech Junction train is about to surrender the single line token for the section from West Pennard to the Evercreech Junction signalman. Two other steam locomotives are in the immediate vicinity: one is almost totally hidden by the signal box whilst another can just be discerned 'blowing off' in the goods yard on the right of the shot beyond the signal box. The locomotive is veteran 3F Class 0-6-0 No.43436 that was constructed for the Midland Railway by Dubs & Co. in 1893, so it was a mere sixty-six years old when this picture was taken. It remained in traffic until June 1962, so it certainly earned its keep! Surprisingly, perhaps, No.43436 was allocated to Rose Grove shed, in Lancashire, at the time of its withdrawal, a far cry from the rural delights of the Highbridge branch! *R.C. Riley*

A Highbridge-bound train rolls into Pylle Halt with Collett-designed 2251 Class 0-6-0 No.2218 in charge. The station buildings here consisted of a combined stationmaster's house and goods shed on the down side, which was an extremely impressive stone-built structure with an attractive façade and porch, while the main building for passenger use was provided on the up side. Remarkably, twenty years after closure its main door was still clearly marked 'Booking Office'. The road overbridge carried the Ilchester to Shepton Mallet (Fosse Way) road over the line.
The station was located more than a mile from the village so it was unlikely to have been busy, and became unstaffed from 4th November 1957. This photograph was taken on 11th July 1964. *Michael Chown*

'You have been sternly warned'. This cast iron S&D notice made it quite clear that trespass on railway property would on no account be tolerated. It was photographed at Pylle on 6th March 1966, the last day the line was operational. *John Beckett*

A further picture taken at Pylle station on the same day as the previous photograph, showing part of the signal box and a rather ornate oil lamp. The seventeen-lever signal box was closed in 1929 when the passing loop was removed but stayed in use as a ground frame controlling the siding that served the goods shed until the siding closed on 10th June 1963. There used to be a lime works at Pylle, located half a mile west of the station, but this was closed prior to the First World War. *Michael Chown*

EVERCREECH JUNCTION TO HIGHBRIDGE AND BURNHAM-ON-SEA

The 4.00pm Highbridge to Evercreech Junction train, formed of a single passenger coach and a van, is depicted at West Pennard station on 28th August 1964. Motive power, once again, is Collett-designed 0-6-0 No.2218, a Swindon product dating from June 1940 which lasted in traffic until November 1964. West Pennard station was situated at the foot of a long bank that descended from Pylle and was also noteworthy due to its position on a section of line that ran dead straight for four miles, this being quite a contrast to the Evercreech Junction to Bath section of the S&D which abounded with tight curves. A large stone-built goods shed was provided at West Pennard, this being situated on a goods loop that ran round the back of the short down platform. The booking office, waiting room and staff accommodation were on the up platform. On 26th August 1964, just two days before the date of this picture, the down passenger loop and sidings were taken out of use, the twenty-three lever signal box being closed from that date. *Alan Reeve*

A brace of Ivatt-designed Class 2MT 2-6-2Ts, Nos.41307 and 41249, head eastwards near Steanbow, between West Pennard and Pylle, with the LCGB 'Somerset & Dorset' rail tour on 5th March 1966. On arrival at Evercreech Junction a pair of Bulleid Pacifics took over for the run to Bath and return. The operating authorities were obviously keen to gather all locomotives remaining on the S&D at Bath shed in order to simplify disposal and No.41307 was diagrammed to pilot the 2.00pm Templecombe to Bath passenger train from Evercreech Junction later in the day while No.41249 was worked back to Bath 'light engine'. *Charles Whetmath*

The last of the mail bags has been loaded, the platform barrow has been cleared out of the way, the locomotive is 'blowing off' impatiently and the driver is looking out anxiously for the 'right away'. How many times has this everyday platform-end scene been enacted over the years? This picture was taken at Glastonbury & Street station on a sunny 5th August 1961 and shows the 1.20pm from Evercreech Junction to Highbridge train awaiting departure behind a real veteran locomotive, a Johnson-designed Class 3F 0-6-0, No.43216, that was one of a small fleet of these engines built for the Somerset & Dorset Joint Railway Company, this particular example being constructed by Neilson & Co. Ltd in 1902. It is thought that No.43216 was the last active survivor, lasting until September 1962. On this particular day, a Saturday during the August Bank Holiday weekend, this train was especially extended through to Burnham-on-Sea for the benefit of day trippers. Glastonbury's twenty-nine lever signal box, which was built in the style of the Midland Railway, is prominent on the left. *David Soggee*

A Collett-designed 2251 Class 0-6-0, No.3216, waits at Glastonbury & Street station with a Highbridge-bound train some time in the early 1960s. The station here was known simply as 'Glastonbury' until July 1886 when it was first advertised with the suffix. The headquarters offices of the S&D were located at Glastonbury from 1861 to 1877. The station was one of the largest on the S&D system with an imposing main building, long platform canopies and a decorative footbridge, the last-mentioned being something of a luxury on the S&D. The premises even boasted a refreshment room – an even greater luxury – but this was closed prior to the Second World War. The down platform was an island, the northern face being used by Wells trains until that branch was closed on 29th October 1951. At the eastern end of the station there was a hut for a gatekeeper who worked the level crossing gates while the commodious goods yard was equipped with two hand cranes, cattle docks and a shed. The arrival of this locomotive on the S&D could have caused some confusion had it happened a decade earlier as it carried the same pre-nationalisation number as the engine seen in the previous picture, which was allocated to Templecombe when carrying '3216'. *Online Transport Archive*

Photographed with the unique and unmistakable landmark of Glastonbury Tor just visible in the background through the mist, Ivatt 2-6-2Ts Nos.41307 and 41249 accelerate the LCGB's 'Somerset & Dorset' rail tour away from its Glastonbury station stop on 5th March 1966. The first-mentioned locomotive is in quite presentable external order but the train engine is rather grubby. The train is formed of a rake of BR Standard and Bulleid coaches in green livery. *Trevor Owen*

The next station after Glastonbury for westbound trains was Ashcott, which was known as 'Ashcott & Meare' until 1876. The station building and stationmaster's house were both built of red brick, the former consisting of only basic facilities comprising of a booking office and waiting room. There was also a tiny ten-lever ground frame (not a block post) controlling the level crossing and its protecting signals and the single siding that comprised the goods yard. The siding was closed from 13th July 1964. Originally there was a wooden platform with wooden paling fencing, but these were replaced by standard Southern Railway-designed concrete and steel components at some stage. This picture was taken on 5th March 1966. *Charles Whetmath*

The area around Ashcott abounded with vast fields of peat and about half a mile west of Ashcott station a two-foot gauge tramway crossed the S&D line on the level. The tramway connected a peat company's works with the nearby peat beds and the works was also served by a siding off the 'main line'. This most unusual feature was also photographed on 5th March 1966. *Charles Whetmath*

The largely low lying, featureless countryside on this section of the S&D line made life difficult for railway photographers and comparatively few pictures taken on the Evercreech Junction to Highbridge route were submitted for publication in this album. In total contrast, the Evercreech to Bath stretch was one of the most rewarding lines in Great Britain! Here, the photographer has obviously used his imagination in order to obtain a worthwhile shot but the intended reflection in South Drain, which runs parallel to the line at this point, has been spoilt by ripples on the surface of the water. The train is the LCGB's farewell special which ran on 5th March 1966. The building in the background is Edington Burtle station, formerly the junction for Bridgwater until that line's closure to passengers in December 1952. In its heyday there were three platforms there, including a bay for the sole use of the branch trains, a loop, and a thirty-nine lever signal box. Most of these lavish facilities were taken out of use in February 1956. *Trevor Owen*

Bason Bridge station was dominated by the adjacent United Dairies milk factory which dated from 1909. Thousands of gallons of milk used to be despatched daily by rail and for this reason a connection to Highbridge was retained until 2nd October 1972. The platform at Bason Bridge was rather narrow, while the meagre passenger facilities were provided by small but neat wooden buildings. In this portrait 4F Class 0-6-0 No.44560 is depicted pausing at Bason Bridge with the Southern Counties Touring Society's 'Southern Wanderer' rail tour on 28th March 1965. This engine was built by the Midland Railway in 1922 for the S&DJR where it was allocated No.60: it became part of LMSR stock in 1930. The river Brue, which flows into the Bristol Channel at Burnham-on-Sea, can be seen on the right. *Roy Hobbs*

A short two-coach train from Evercreech Junction, hauled by Ivatt Class 2MT 2-6-2T No.41296, coasts past Highbridge East 'C' signal box some time in the early 1960s. For most of its career this twenty-five lever signal box was known as Highbridge Loco Box and was responsible for movements at the eastern end of the station and those to the locomotive works (prior to its closure) and two-road engine shed. After nationalisation BR embarked on a programme of renaming signal boxes in the immediate environs of Highbridge, and this box was renamed Highbridge East 'C', remaining in use until the end. There used to be a carriage shed immediately behind the box but this disappeared many years ago. *Colour-Rail*

EVERCREECH JUNCTION TO HIGHBRIDGE AND BURNHAM-ON-SEA

Another picture of a train from Evercreech Junction entering Highbridge station but this time with really vintage motive power. The locomotive is yet another 'old timer', MR 3F Class 0-6-0 No.43593, which was built by Kitson & Co. and entered traffic in January 1900. This machine spent the last years of its life in the Bristol area being allocated to Barrow Road shed for a long period during the 1950s. It remained in service until October 1962 when it was withdrawn from Gloucester shed and eventually broken-up in June 1963. This picture dates from August 1960. *Colour-Rail*

The 4.00pm train to Templecombe, with 2251 Class 0-6-0 No.3210 in charge, awaits departure from Highbridge on 18th August 1963. There were two terminating tracks at Highbridge station, one of which was one of the few examples in this country with a platform on both sides – a most interesting feature. The other bay platform is behind the train and apparently occupied by berthed rolling stock. The two through platforms, formerly used by trains to and from Burnham-on-Sea, can be clearly seen on the left of the picture. Note the old Highbridge 'A' signal box at the end of the platform: this had been out of use since 1914. Part of the GWR signal box, which controlled movements on the main line, can also be discerned. The principal station building on the S&D side of the premises was located adjacent to Platform One and its roof can be seen above the carriages. It was an attractive building built of brick with stone window surrounds and quoins (cornerstones). There was a bronze memorial to the Highbridge staff who died during the First World War. At the time of this picture there were half a dozen weekday trains in each direction along the Highbridge branch but this number was reduced to two when BR introduced a special emergency service in January 1966. The footbridge gave access to the GWR main line platforms which are out of sight on the left. *Colour-Rail*

The last day of passenger trains at Highbridge. The LCGB's farewell special poses there on 5th March 1966, the final day of public passenger trains in the former S&D part of the station. Mourners gather round Ivatt 2-6-2Ts Nos.41307 and 41249, no doubt mindful that they would never again travel from Evercreech Junction to this rather bleak and windswept outpost of the S&D system. Highbridge was formerly an important intermediate station on the Somerset Central Railway's main line and this probably accounts for the five platforms that were originally provided. In more recent times, and particularly following the withdrawal of passenger services on the branch to Burnham in 1951, the lavish layout here was hardly justified by the amount of traffic on offer and it seems incredible that no rationalisation occurred: Highbridge S&D platforms almost became a 'forgotten' area of the station. The buildings which are partially visible in the background on the right are the ruins of the old Highbridge Works which was closed in 1930 with the loss of 300 jobs. This must have been a shattering blow for the townsfolk at a time of considerable economic hardship. Despite closure many years previously these structures were still standing at the time of the line's demise. *Roy Hobbs*

EVERCREECH JUNCTION TO HIGHBRIDGE AND BURNHAM-ON-SEA

In this illustration GWR 2251 Class No.2204 is negotiating the very tight curve off the Burnham-on-Sea branch that led onto the down main line at Highbridge. Not many places had such remarkably complicated trackwork, this being an aspect of railways that considerably added to their fascination. The GWR goods yard can be seen in the distance, with the shed prominent. Note the wonderful mixture of SR and GWR signals, those on the extreme left being particularly interesting. This shot was also taken on 18th August 1963. *Colour-Rail*

An exceptionally rare colour view of a passenger train at Burnham-on-Sea. The line from Highbridge to Burnham was closed to passengers as long ago as 29th October 1951 but excursion trains continued in the summer months until 8th September 1962. In this photograph 3F Class 0-6-0 No.43216 is seen waiting to leave for Highbridge with the empty coaches of the 1.20pm from Evercreech Junction on 5th August 1961. This train had been especially extended to Burnham for day trippers. The return passenger train for the excursionists left Burnham at 7.00pm and on arrival at Highbridge formed the advertised 7.10pm service to Evercreech Junction, arrival there being at 8.09pm. The original terminus at Burnham-on-Sea had an all-over roof, which gave the station a very gloomy interior, and a short platform on the eastern end of which stood a small signal cabin. A longer excursion platform was later added to accommodate lengthy holiday trains, this being clearly visible in the foreground. The line continued beyond the station to a jetty, the rails here reputedly being used at one time to launch the local lifeboat! *David Soggee*

Cole's unpretentious buildings suggest that this modest, wayside station was of no particular significance but, in reality, nothing could be further from the truth. This location is one of considerable historical importance because the lines of the Dorset Central and Somerset Central railways met just north of here in 1862. The two companies had already agreed to join forces and operate as one unified system and – later the same year – they amalgamated to form the celebrated Somerset & Dorset Railway. In this illustration former GWR Collett 0-6-0 No.3206 draws to a halt with the 4.00pm Highbridge to Templecombe local train on 18th August 1962. Note the person perched atop the bracket signal on the up line. He is the late Ivo Peters, a superbly artistic and skilful photographer, who specialised in taking pictures along the S&D line. *Colour-Rail*

A further view of Cole station (29¼ miles from Bath), this time showing the 1.10pm Bath to Templecombe local train waiting to leave behind BR Standard Class 3MT 2-6-2T No.82041 on 6th November 1965. Locomotives of this class were introduced on the S&D by the Western Region after it gained control of part of the route in 1958 and representatives of this class were based at both Bath and Templecombe sheds. In addition to working stopping services along the S&D route they were also used on similar trains over the former Midland Railway line to Bristol (Temple Meads). This particular locomotive was the last member of its class active on the S&D line, being withdrawn in December 1965. The stone-built station buildings at Cole, located on the down platform, were of typical Dorset Central Railway design with high gables and tall chimneys but no canopy. There was a wooden waiting shelter on the up platform. The small goods yard closed on 5th April 1965 while the fourteen-lever wooden signal box, also on the up side, was shut at the end of May 1965. *Michael Allen*

Between Cole and Wincanton the S&D passed through some of the loveliest, unspoilt countryside on the route, to which this illustration bears ample testament. The train depicted is the 8.15am Bath to Templecombe 'local', hauled by BR Standard Class 5MT No.73049 which is seen passing the tiny hamlet of Pitcombe on 13th June 1964. Could one wish for a more attractive backdrop to a railway photograph? *John Beckett*

Another picture of the 8.15am Bath to Templecombe train near Pitcombe, this time taken on 17th July 1965. The motive power is provided by an unidentified BR Standard Class 4MT 2-6-4T locomotive. In complete contrast to the section north of Evercreech Junction, this part of the route was easily graded with the line rising gently towards Wincanton at this point but this is unlikely to have troubled one of these powerful 2-6-4Ts with a lightweight three-coach load. *John Beckett*

Utter frustration at Shepton Montague! How many times has a railway photographer been waiting in glorious sunshine only for it to disappear behind a cloud at the critical moment? The sun is shining brightly on the fields just a few hundred yards from where the photographer was standing but not, unfortunately, on the subject of the photograph. The train is the 10.55am SO Manchester Piccadilly to Bournemouth West with BR Standard Class 4MT No.75027 assisting Bulleid 'West Country' Pacific No.34040 *Crewkerne* and this picture was taken on 25th August 1962. Even so, despite the sun's lack of cooperation a pleasing image has resulted. A picture of this train leaving Bath (taken in sun!) appears elsewhere in this album. *John Beckett*

The 7.00am Cleethorpes to Exmouth train is depicted passing Shepton Montague on 18th August 1962. Motive power is provided by BR Standard Class 4MT 4-6-0 No.75009 piloting S&D Class 7F 2-8-0 No.53810. Note how the lines diverged prior to passing under Rock Cutting bridge which is seen in the next photograph. Judging by the extremely wide cutting at this point a lot of spoil seems to have been excavated for use in building the long embankment just north of here. No.53810 achieved the unfortunate distinction of being the first of the later batch of these engines to be withdrawn, an event which occurred in December 1963. *Colour-Rail*

The 12.20pm Bournemouth to Nottingham train, in charge of unrebuilt Bulleid 'West Country' Pacific No.34103 *Calstock,* passes beneath bridge No.127, near Shepton Montague, on 1st September 1962. *Calstock* was a refugee from the South Eastern Section where it worked for the first part of its career, based for a time at Dover shed. When steam traction was displaced by electrification No.34103 found employment at Bournemouth depot from where it was operating at the time of this photograph. The bridge, which carried a country lane from Shepton Montague to Stoke across the railway, was known locally as Rock Cutting Bridge. It had an exceptionally high clearance, the height from rail level to the soffits being a remarkable 21ft. 2in. in complete contrast to many other structures on the line that were notable for their extremely limited clearances. *R.C. Riley*

Rock Cutting Bridge is seen again, this time on a sunny 12th September 1962, with Collett 2251 Class 0-6-0 No.2204 passing beneath the relatively lofty structure with the 4.00pm Highbridge to Templecombe local train. These locomotives were, needless to say, completely alien to the S&D and were only introduced at a very late stage in the history of the line, after the WR obtained control of most of the route in 1958. The first recorded working of a 2251 Class engine along the line occurred on 31st March 1960 when No.3218 powered a Templecombe to Blandford Forum pick-up goods train, this reportedly being the first appearance of a Great Western-designed locomotive south of Templecombe since 'Bulldogs' worked Weston-super-Mare to Bournemouth excursions prior to the Second World War! The WR even experimented, apparently, with 5600 Class 0-6-2Ts on coal trains between Bath and collieries in the Radstock area. On 4th December 1959 No.6641 passed through Radstock with coal empties for Norton Hill colliery, returning later the same morning with a loaded coal train. No further sorties of these engines on the S&D line were reported, so presumably the 5600 Class engines did not quite match the superb characteristics of the S&D Class 7Fs which were specially designed for the route! *John Beckett*

EVERCREECH JUNCTION TO WINCANTON

A peaceful, pastoral scene about a mile north of Wincanton, showing the 1.10pm Bath to Templecombe train ambling along behind BR Standard Class 5MT 4-6-0 No.73051. This photograph was taken on 11th July 1964. The milk tank wagons were doubtless *en route* from the creamery at Bason Bridge, near Highbridge, to Templecombe for onward movement to London and would have been attached to the train at Evercreech Junction. This substantial traffic, including the 4.19pm Highbridge to Templecombe milk train, was later re-routed by the Western Region in order to strengthen the case for closure. *Michael Chown*

The shadows are lengthening as LMSR Class 8F 2-8-0 No.48760 accelerates away from its Wincanton station stop with the three-coach 4.18pm Templecombe to Bath stopping train on 5th March 1966. This was the final northbound public passenger train run on the S&D in daylight, the last train of all being the 6.46pm Bournemouth to Bath service which was due off Templecombe at 8.20pm. The latter working was hauled by a brace of BR Standard Class 4MT 2-6-4Ts, Nos.80041 and 80043. The sad events of that weekend drew crowds from all over Great Britain and the last public train to Bath was packed to the gunwhales with people making their last trip over the line. A coffin was ceremoniously put on board at Evercreech Junction. *Trevor Owen*

BR Standard Class 9F 2-10-0 No.92220 *Evening Star* accelerates away from its Wincanton station stop with the 3.40pm Bournemouth to Bristol train on 18th August 1962. This train, known to staff on the S&D as the 'Up Mail', had priority over all other traffic – including the 'Pines Express' – because it connected at Mangotsfield with an evening mail train from Bristol to the north of England. On 8th September 1962 *Evening Star* hauled the last 'Pines Express' over the S&D in both directions, the up train, which comprised of twelve coaches and weighed 426 tons, being the heaviest load ever taken over the line unassisted. What better tribute to the capability of these locomotives, not to mention the phenomenal hard work of the fireman, could there be? *Michael Allen*

In 1960 the 7.00am Cleethorpes to Exmouth train (and corresponding return working) which loaded to only ten bogies, was invariably rostered for a S&D Class 7F 2-8-0 between Bath and Templecombe: this obviated the need for an assisting engine across the Mendips. SR motive power was used between Templecombe and Exmouth and vice versa. By 1961, however, the number of S&D 2-8-0s capable of hauling passenger trains was down to five and, consequently, the above-mentioned services were often booked for a Class 4F 0-6-0 piloted by a Class 2P 4-4-0. By the summer of the following year circumstances had again changed and BR Standard Class 4MT 4-6-0s had ousted the faithful 2Ps from piloting work. In this portrait the 7.00am from Cleethorpes is seen approaching Wincanton behind the rather unlikely combination of LMSR Class 4F No.44411, piloted by BR Standard 4-6-0 No.75009 on 1st September 1962. Note the unorthodox position of the train reporting number on the front mainframes of the leading engine. *Michael Allen*

Opposite below: The S&D line was well provided with turntables and, judging by the pictures submitted for publication in this album, tender-first running was quite rare. Perhaps No.75073, seen here at the same spot as the previous picture, was a last-minute substitute for a defective locomotive. The train is the 3.05pm Templecombe to Evercreech 'local' and this portrait was taken on 1st September 1962. *Michael Allen*

The down 'Pines Express' nears Wincanton on 1st September 1962 with Bulleid 'West Country' Pacific No.34043 *Combe Martin,* a regular performer on the S&D line, in charge. The locomotive is in a decidedly neglected condition and, indeed, 1962 proved to be No.34043's last full year in traffic. In June of the following year it was transferred from Bournemouth shed to the WR (at least on paper) and apparently immediately withdrawn from service together with Nos.34035, 34055 and 34074. In August 1963 *Combe Martin* arrived at Eastleigh Works and was broken-up in mid-September, becoming the first Bulleid Pacific to suffer this fate. *Michael Allen*

Wincanton station (33½ miles from Bath), with its distinctive partially staggered platforms, is seen in this shot taken on 6th November 1965. The northbound up platform was considerably longer than the southbound one. The usual passenger facilities were provided on the down side, the up side platform merely having a simple shelter similar to those provided at other S&D stations. There was a lot of goods traffic here because, in addition to regular livestock traffic, Wincanton dealt with a large number of horse boxes in connection with the local races. Goods shipments increased markedly in 1933 when extra sidings were laid to serve a Cow & Gate factory from where a substantial quantity of milk tank wagons was despatched to London on a daily basis. Another fascinating aspect of Wincanton was the fact that it was one of the first stations on the S&D line to be illuminated by gas, the equipment apparently being ordered by the Dorset Central Railway in 1862. *Michael Allen*

Some time during the spring of 1963 one of Bath (Green Park) shed's stud of BR Standard Class 5MT locomotives, No.73049, was involved in a minor collision and ran around for at least three months with a buckled running plate. Here it is seen leaving Wincanton station with a train to Bournemouth West in early July 1963 with the damage clearly visible. A few days later it was summoned to Eastleigh Works for a heavy repair and emerged in late September resplendent in fully lined-out green livery with its 'disfigurement' fully repaired. *Alan Reeve*

Most extensive engineering work on the S&D took place on Sundays when traffic was comparatively light: indeed, no trains at all were advertised on Sundays during the winter period. In this illustration S&D 2-8-0 Class 7F No.53810 simmers at Wincanton on Sunday 16th July 1961 with an engineer's train which included a staff coach of LMSR design that had a 'SC' prefix, indicating it was supposedly based on the Scottish Region! In the summer 1961 timetable three trains were scheduled in each direction so the engineers would not have had the line entirely to themselves. The service, as might be expected at a time before private motoring became the norm for the masses, was clearly designed for day trippers – from the Bristol and Bath areas, and some of the busier intermediate stations – who wished to spend a day beside the sea at Bournemouth. There were departures from Bath at 9.30am and 10.05am, the latter being a through working from Bristol Temple Meads. The next southbound train, again a through train from Bristol, left Bath at 7.47pm. In the opposite direction there was a morning train up from Bournemouth and then nothing until two departures left in quick succession after 7.00pm, one of which went through to Bristol. Wincanton was especially noteworthy because it retained some of its rather tall lower quadrant signals with wooden arms until closure. *R.C. Riley*

WINCANTON TO TEMPLECOMBE

Templecombe, like Halwill, Tebay and Woodford Halse, was a railway junction of considerable importance which was out of all proportion to the otherwise somewhat insignificant place it served. The S&D line, running roughly north to south, passed underneath the main SR Waterloo to Exeter route at Templecombe and the two lines were connected by a spur which gave S&D trains access to the main line station. The spur line left the S&D 'main line' at Templecombe No.2 Junction and ran into a platform at Templecombe station that provided a direct connection with the SR main line but, in reality, apart from one or two seasonal workings, it was used exclusively as a bay platform by S&D services. The method of operation for S&D trains calling at Templecombe was quite fascinating. Down trains ran straight into the S&D platform at Templecombe station and would have a pilot engine attached to the other end of the train. When it was time to depart the pilot locomotive would head the train backwards to a point just north of No.2 Junction where it would be detached and the train would then set off towards Bournemouth. Northbound trains came to a halt at No.2 Junction where another engine would be coupled to the rear and draw the train backwards into the main line station. This would then be uncoupled and when it was time to leave the train would proceed on its way towards Bath with the train engine once again in charge. In this scene, photographed on 6th September 1963, Collett 2251 Class 0-6-0 No.2247 (just visible in the distance) pulls a Bournemouth to Bath local train backwards into Templecombe station, while train engine No.92224 remains on the front end throughout the entire manoeuvre. Just the kind of performance that made the study of railways so wonderfully rewarding in past years! *Alan Reeve*

The last 'Pines Express' over the S&D was scheduled to run on 8th September 1962, and BR Standard Class 9F No.92220 *Evening Star* was temporarily transferred to Bath (Green Park) shed on 8th August to work this train because it was felt appropriate that the last steam locomotive built for BR should haul the final 'Pines Express' over the Mendips. Its first appearance on the 'Pines' was on 11th August and after the momentous events of 8th September, when No.92220 gave a record-breaking performance, the engine was moved away from Bath on 13th September. Almost a year later, however, No.92220 returned to Green Park depot! In August 1963 Bath shed was short of motive power and requested the loan of two Class 5MT locomotives but, no doubt to the total surprise of many staff, it was sent two Class 9Fs instead, Nos.92220 *Evening Star* and 92224. These engines were hardly suited to the short local trains then being operated and, furthermore, the 9Fs were unnecessarily heavy on coal; also their length precluded their use on goods trains because they were too long for the Evercreech Junction turntable. So they were put to use on three-coach 'locals' from Bath to Bournemouth which hardly constituted an exacting task for locomotives of such power. In this picture, recorded on the same day as the previous shot, a rather travel-stained No.92220 passes Templecombe lower yard with a local train to Bournemouth. What a waste of a jolly good engine! *Alan Reeve*

LMSR Class 2P 4-4-0 No.40569, in charge of a train bound for Bournemouth, has been given the 'right away' following its Templecombe station stop and is drawn back along the spur line to No.2 Junction by an unidentified locomotive at the other end of the train. The pilot engine will then be uncoupled thus enabling No.40569 to continue its journey to the coast. Note the very tight curvature of the spur line at this point. The main Waterloo to Exeter platforms are behind the photographer. *Colour-Rail*

When the S&D came under the jurisdiction of the Western Region in 1958 they attempted to 'Westernise' the line and, as a result, 2251 Class locomotives and pannier tank engines became commonplace, especially on the Highbridge branch and south of Templecombe where the gradients were not so severe. The WR even tried to introduce 5600 Class 0-6-2Ts (as previously stated), but the trials came to nothing. Here, on a dull 28th March 1964, 5700 Class 0-6-0PT No.4634 sits outside Templecombe shed with another, unidentified member of the class alongside. The smoke-blackened shed walls mask the fact that it is of quite recent construction, being built in 1950. Clearly, at that time the railway authorities saw a long-term future for the S&D line – what a pity their optimism was not justified by events.
Michael Chown

Templecombe shed on 1st January 1966, the last day of normal scheduled services. A shaft of sunlight momentarily shines through a chink in the otherwise leaden sky and beautifully illuminates a BR Standard Class 4MT 4-6-0 and a pair of Ivatt Class 2MT 2-6-2Ts standing awaiting their next duties. The engines nearest to the camera are thought to be Nos.75078 and 41307. Note the rather primitive locomotive coaling arrangements.
Trevor Owen

TEMPLECOMBE MOTIVE POWER DEPOT

A roadbridge that took Combe Throop Lane across the S&D line also gave a grandstand view of activity on the locomotive shed, not that there seems to be much happening in this picture taken on 7th July 1959. The Class 4F 0-6-0 standing next to the old Dorset Central buildings is No.44422, while BR Standard Class 5MT No.73047 and S&D Class 7F No.53804 can be seen in the background. The most prominent engines, however, are two LMSR Class 2P 4-4-0s, both of which appear to be stored out of use. No.40537, nearest to the camera, is something of a mystery engine. It appears to have been officially allocated to Bristol (Barrow Road) shed at the time of this photograph and remained so until it was reallocated to Templecombe in March 1962. On 22nd August 1962 No.40537 worked into Bath *en route* to Derby Works for cutting-up and left on its melancholy journey the following morning. At least it achieved a degree of fame as the last representative of its type to work over the S&D. Strangely, however, the author has never seen any pictures of this locomotive in revenue-earning service on the line, so it is questionable whether No.40537 worked regularly over the route – a curious case! *R.C.Riley*

TEMPLECOMBE MOTIVE POWER DEPOT

The 4.16pm Evercreech Junction to Bournemouth train, powered by LMSR Class 4F 0-6-0 No.44559, which is in quite polished external condition, accelerates downhill from No.2 Junction past Templecombe shed on 12th July 1960. This picture, which was presumably taken from atop a signal post, provides a splendid panoramic view of the various routes that converged on this tiny Somerset village and the railway installations that were subsequently constructed. The tracks in the right foreground led into Templecombe station, whilst the Waterloo to Exeter main line runs along an embankment in the middle distance. The modern brick-built engine shed dominates the left-hand side of the shot, whilst beyond it is the stone-built former Dorset Central Railway stationmaster's house which marks the location of the original S&D Templecombe station that was closed in 1887. Templecombe Lower platform can also be discerned between the roadbridge and the bridge that carries the main line over the S&D's single track. *R.C. Riley*

The area around Templecombe was blanketed by snow when this shot of LMSR-designed Class 2MT 2-6-2T No.41208 pulling (what appears to be) a goods working was taken on 6th March 1965. The locomotive is passing Templecombe Lower platform which is almost totally hidden by a considerable covering of snow. The platform was located between two bridges, the structure in the background being a roadbridge carrying a local lane whilst the Waterloo to West-of-England line passed over the S&D on a bridge immediately behind the photographer. *Colin Caddy*

Opposite lower: This portrait of Henstridge station, looking towards Templecombe, was taken on 5th September 1964 and by this date the station's paintwork was rather faded. The bridge in the background carried the Sherborne to Shaftesbury road across the line. The goods yard here was closed from 5th April 1965. *Colin Caddy*

TEMPLECOMBE TO STALBRIDGE

Above: Henstridge station (38½ miles from Bath) was one of the smallest on the S&D line, the platform being a mere 150 feet long. It was the first station on the 16 miles-long stretch of single line from Templecombe to Blandford Forum but Henstridge had no passing loop nor signal box. The buildings were a mixture of brick and wooden construction and housed the ladies' and gentlemen's waiting rooms, booking office and toilets. The tiny goods yard consisted of one siding, controlled by a ground frame, and there was a cattle pen and milk dock. The uninspiring station frontage is seen in this shot which was taken on 6th November 1965. *Michael Allen*

Above right: Memories of the bygone age of the country railway. A cattle pen, water trough and rather elegant, slender lamp standard with its oil burner are reminders of times past when small rural communities depended on the railway for the movement of passengers, goods and farm produce including, of course, livestock. This quiet corner of Henstridge station was recorded on 2nd June 1961. *Alan Jarvis*

Stalbridge station (40¼ miles from Bath) on New Year's Day 1966. The S&D line was originally scheduled for closure from 3rd January 1966, but this had to be deferred for a couple of months because a bus operator unexpectedly withdrew his application for a licence to provide one of the replacement services. BR grudgingly provided an 'interim emergency service' for a further period until the arrangements for the substitute road services were finalised. On 1st January 1966 many enthusiasts descended on the line for the last day of 'normal' services and some are seen here on the up platform as BR Standard Class 4MT 2-6-4T No.80043, in charge of the 12.23pm Templecombe to Bournemouth, waits to cross the 11.40am *ex*-Bournemouth. *Colin Caddy*

Photographed near Stalbridge on a sunny 28th March 1965, BR Standard Class 5MT 4-6-0 No.73022 heads for Templecombe with the Southern Counties Touring Society's 'Southern Wanderer' rail tour. This train started from London's Victoria station and travelled down the Mid Sussex Line, between Horsham and Arundel Junction, before continuing via Fareham and Bournemouth to Templecombe – quite an ingenious route! The participants were then treated to a trip along the Highbridge branch, powered by Fowler Class 4F 0-6-0 No.44560, before returning to Templecombe. On arrival there Bulleid 'Merchant Navy' Pacific No.35023 *Holland-Afrika Line* took over for the run back to the capital. *Roy Hobbs*

Despite the fact that it passed through some very appealing rolling Dorset countryside, the southern part of the S&D never seemed to attract enthusiasts in the same way as the hilly section north of Evercreech Junction. Just north of Sturminster Newton the line crossed over the river Stour at a wonderfully photogenic rural location but, judging by the paucity of pictures submitted for inclusion in this album, regrettably very few photographs seem to have been taken here. In this portrait BR Standard Class 9F No.92220 *Evening Star* rumbles across the girder bridge over the river with the 3.40pm Bournemouth West to Bristol train on 1st September 1962. The photographer no doubt hoped for a better reflection but luck was not on his side on this occasion! *R.C. Riley*

The S&D was noted for the extremely restricted nature of most bridges and tunnels, most notably the very low and narrow tunnels just south of Bath. Obviously its accountants held sway when the line was being built, just as they did, sadly, when it was closed. In this illustration the 'Pines Express', seen entering Sturminster Newton (44¼ miles from Bath) on 1st September 1962, only just manages to squeeze beneath the exceptionally low road overbridge north of the station. Motive power is provided by Bulleid 'West Country' Pacific No.34043 *Combe Martin* which appears to be in rather run-down condition. The principal station facilities were on the up side here: there was only a basic waiting shelter on the down side. The small goods yard contained a cattle dock, seven-ton hand crane and a fair-sized shed which is partially concealed by the locomotive in this picture: there was also a siding that served the local dairy. The yard was closed from 5th April 1965. *R.C. Riley*

An unidentified Ivatt Class 2MT 2-6-2T runs into the down loop at Sturminster Newton on 15th June 1965. The train is thought to be the 3.35pm Templecombe to Blandford Forum passenger train which continued to Bailey Gate as empty coaching stock – hence the (presumably empty) milk tanks in the formation. After collecting milk tanks from the sidings there the locomotive worked back to Templecombe as the 4.46pm Bailey Gate to Templecombe milk train, consequently the passenger coaches would not have been available for public use. Note that the layout was designed to give up trains a clear run through the station, this being true of all stations on the single-line section south of Templecombe. A distinctive feature of Sturminster Newton was the pronounced dip in the platform, there being no footbridge at the station, and this made it easier for passengers to cross the line over the boarded crossing. *Online Transport Archive*

Shillingstone station (47¼ miles from Bath) is seen in this portrait that was taken on 6th November 1965. The station was well known for its attractive garden on the up platform which, judging by this picture, seems to have been well kept right up to closure. Another feature of Shillingstone station was the platform awning that was reputedly provided for the benefit of King Edward VII, who was a regular visitor to the nearby Iwerne Minster House. The main passenger facilities here were on the up side in a brick-built station building, the down platform having only a basic waiting shelter. The tiny goods yard was also on the up side and boasted a five-ton hand crane, a small shed and a loading dock.
Michael Allen

Shillingstone station's brightly-painted green and cream sixteen-lever signal box is prominent in this view which was recorded on 15th June 1965. BR Standard Class 5MT 4-6-0 No.73051 pauses with an up stopping train formed of three coaches and a van. The station was located close to the river Stour which is just out of the picture on the left. *Online Transport Archive*

STALBRIDGE TO SHILLINGSTONE

Rolling chalk downs provide a splendid backdrop and puffy clouds scud across the sky as BR Standard Class 3MT 2-6-2T No.82002 coasts along between Blandford Forum and Shillingstone with an up local train. The location is thought to be Cliff Bridge, about two miles south of Shillingstone, and this lovely rural scene was recorded on 24th August 1962. The land on the left rises to Hod Hill, one of the many Roman forts and settlements in the area. Part of the village of Stourpaine is just discernible in the distance. At the time of this picture, four of these Swindon-built locomotives were based on the S&D, Nos.82001/2 at Templecombe and Nos.82004/41 at Bath (Green Park). *Colour-Rail*

Bulleid 'Merchant Navy' Pacific No.35011 *General Steam Navigation* has just crossed the river Stour (note the bridge in the background) and makes a splendid sight as it rushes up the Stour valley with a RCTS rail tour. It was photographed between Blandford Forum and Shillingstone on 1st January 1966. Locomotives of this class were officially banned from the S&D line, but with closure imminent the BR hierarchy was apparently unconcerned and No.35011 became the first of two 'Merchant Navy' Class engines to work over the southern section of the line. *Roger Merry-Price*

Blandford Forum station (52³/₄ miles from Bath), seen here on 24th April 1965, was the largest intermediate traffic centre between Templecombe and Broadstone, and judged to merit the luxury of a subway. A large brick station building was provided on the up platform together with a commodious canopy. The signalman here surveyed train movements from a very tall, twenty-seven lever signal box on the down platform which dominated that side and, arguably, the entire station. In 1893 this structure replaced an earlier signal box that had been located on the up platform. The first station in the town was called 'Blandford St. Mary', this being replaced in August 1863 by the station depicted here which was initially called 'Blandford' until renamed 'Blandford Forum' in 1953. There was a reasonably-sized goods yard on the down side with the usual facilities. A very short-lived branch, that diverged just south of the station, used to run into the local army camp. This line opened in January 1919 but was apparently out of use within two years, and track removal occurred in 1928 so it did not last very long! The train just visible in the background appears to be a Bailey Gate to Templecombe milk working. *Colin Caddy*

Both platforms are occupied, so this constitutes a busy scene at least by the modest standards of Blandford Forum! In this portrait, taken on 17th August 1963, BR Standard Class 9F 2-10-0 No.92220 *Evening Star* simmers prior to leaving with the 3.40pm Bournemouth to Bristol, which was known as the 'Up Mail'. This train connected at Mangotsfield, as previously mentioned, with a mail train from Bristol to the north of England. This picture was taken during *Evening Star*'s second spell of duty on the S&D when it was sent to Green Park shed with No.92224 to alleviate a motive power shortage. The train in the down platform is unidentified, but is almost certainly the 3.35pm Templecombe to Blandford Forum 'local' which later ran empty to Bailey Gate to collect milk tanks before working back to Templecombe. Note it is waiting for the 'road' at the far end of the platform. The latter is the kind of working that made the study of railways so absolutely fascinating. *Colour-Rail*

The superb, panoramic view from Blandford Forum's signal box, partially visible above the train, can be imagined in this picture of the south end of the station, taken on 7th July 1962. GWR 5700 Class pannier tank locomotive No.3758 is seen awaiting departure with the 12.23pm Templecombe to Bournemouth train. The coaches making up the train are Bulleid-designed vehicles built by the Birmingham Railway Carriage & Wagon Company and running as Set No.969. *Colin Caddy*

The rather drab station buildings at Bailey Gate (59 miles from Bath) are illustrated in this picture which was taken from a stationary train on 6th November 1965. These buildings were on the down side, while passengers waiting for up trains were catered for by a wooden waiting shelter. The station here was originally known as Sturminster Marshall (it was located in the village of that name) but when Sturminster Newton station opened in August 1863 its name was changed to avoid confusion. *Michael Allen*

Many of the illustrations in this album feature outstanding country landscapes as a backcloth, but here the somewhat less appealing United Dairies installation at Bailey Gate forms the background. At least the dairy, established in 1919 when sidings were laid to serve Carters and Dorset Modern Dairies, brought considerable business to the railway. The milk at first travelled to London via Wimborne but was re-routed in 1933 to travel via Templecombe. This shot shows GWR Class 5700 0-6-0PT No.4691 on 25th June 1961, and judging by the fact that it is standing on the down line whilst facing north, suggests that it may have been working a milk train (which is likely to have included passenger stock) heading for Templecombe. *Colour-Rail*

A down goods train, headed by Class 4F 0-6-0 No.44557, waits at Bailey Gate on 4th July 1961. The fireman is standing in the tender presumably shovelling coal forward. This locomotive was one of five engines of this class built by the Midland Railway for the S&D by Armstrong Whitworth & Co. in 1922, their original numbers being 57 to 61. They became part of LMSR stock in 1930 and this particular locomotive remained in traffic until September 1962. *R. C. Riley*

The 'Southern Wanderer' rail tour, with BR Standard 4-6-0 No.73022 in charge, rounds the curve at Corfe Mullen Junction on 28th March 1965. This is the spot where the original line to Wimborne (closed in 1933 apart from a mile-long stub to a private siding) diverged from the route to Broadstone. The Wimborne line was part of the S&D 'main line' from Burnham-on-Sea until the direct route to Broadstone was brought into use in 1885 and this obviated the need for inconvenient, time-consuming reversals at Wimborne station. The line to Wimborne rapidly declined in status following the opening of the Broadstone route and it lost its passenger service from 11th July 1920, but goods workings lasted until 1933. The line seen here is double track, which applied all of the way from Blandford Forum, but this became two separate single lines just beyond Corfe Mullen signal box and level crossing which are just discernible in the distance. The twenty-four lever box here was built in 1905 to control the junction. *Colin Caddy*

BR Standard Class 4MT 2-6-0 No.76010 nears Broadstone with a Templecombe to Bournemouth local train, formed of a set of three Bulleid coaches, on an overcast 30th October 1965. The train is drifting down the 1 in 97 gradient that applied for the final mile or so into Broadstone station. This locomotive was constructed in February 1953 at Horwich works in Lancashire and survived in service until September 1966. *John Beckett*

BR Standard Class 9F 2-10-0 No.92233 draws the northbound 'Pines Express' through Broadstone station on 7th September 1962. The last run of one of these fine locomotives over the S&D in normal service took place on 20th June 1964 when No.92214 powered the 9.55am train from Bath to Bournemouth and returned on the 3.40pm *ex*-Bournemouth, the 'Up Mail'. This station was originally opened by the London & South Western Railway on 1st June 1847 and was part of the Brockenhurst to Dorchester line promoted by Mr. A.L. Castleman, a Wimborne solicitor. Due to its sinuous nature, this route is often referred to as 'Castleman's Corkscrew'. The tracks of the original line to Hamworthy Junction are out of sight on the left of the picture. The S&D route came along twenty-five years later and whereas the original line had a straight run through the station, trains from Bournemouth had to negotiate two awkward curves at the north end in order to reach the S&D's tracks. The first of these curves is clearly visible beyond the footbridge. Train movements at the station were controlled by a thirty-two lever signal box which is the brick-built building just discernible in the background. *John Beckett*

Opposite: An unidentified southbound train swings off the S&D line at Broadstone (63½ miles from Bath) on 7th September 1962. Motive power is provided by BR Standard Class 5MT 4-6-0 No.73049. The line on the right of the picture is the route to Wimborne, Brockenhurst and Salisbury. Immediately after the two routes merged the line to Hamworthy diverged from the route to Bournemouth, hence the junction signal in the background. This junction marked the end of the S&D's own tracks. *John Beckett*

A porter stands transfixed as S&D Class 7F 2-8-0 No.53808 takes a northbound train through Broadstone station in August 1959. S&D line trains ran to (what later became) Hamworthy goods depot until 1874 when a new line was built from Broadstone to Holes Bay Junction, thus giving trains a really worthwhile, direct route to Poole and Bournemouth. During its career Broadstone station has been known as 'New Poole Junction' and 'Broadstone Junction'. *Colour-Rail*

The last day of timetabled passenger services on the S&D line was Saturday 5th March 1966; however, the line was opened especially the following day for two enthusiasts' special trains. A farewell rail tour from London Waterloo was organised by the Railway Correspondence & Travel Society (RCTS) whilst the Stephenson Locomotive Society's (SLS) special was a less ambitious affair and ran from Bath to Bournemouth and back with a diesel multiple unit connection to and from Birmingham. The arrangements for these trains were no doubt complicated by engineering works at Radstock, where a new connection to the former GWR Bristol to Frome line was being installed, and the destruction of Evercreech Junction signal box, which had been gutted by fire the previous evening. Here, a local police constable keeps a watchful eye on the proceedings as the SLS special, hauled by Nos.48706 and 80043 in double harness, sets off on its 71 mile-long run to Bournemouth. *Trevor Owen*

Below: The high embankment and long, straight stretch of track (at least by S&D standards!) at Shepton Montague – not to mention the lovely backdrop – is the unmistakable location for this shot of the southbound SLS special. Note the train is formed of a uniform rake of ten Mk.1 vehicles all in maroon livery which adds to the appeal of the picture. *Trevor Owen*

The RCTS special train commenced its journey in London behind Bulleid 'Merchant Navy' Pacific No.35028 *Clan Line* which powered it from Waterloo to Templecombe via Staines, Woking and Broadstone. No.35028 is depicted passing a group of onlookers at Henstridge station. Note that *Clan Line*, which appears to be in rather grubby condition, has had a wreath affixed to its smokebox door. *Trevor Owen*

6TH MARCH 1966 – THE LAST DAY OF OPERATION

In the period leading up to the closure of the S&D line BR pursued a ruthless policy of removing all assets 'surplus to requirements', as exemplified here by this depressing picture of the RCTS rail tour passing the remains of the marshalling yard at Evercreech Junction on 6th March. It is sad to reflect that this once-busy yard was the hub of freight operations on the S&D system but by the date of this picture it had been almost completely erased from the landscape. What a terrible sight! The tour was *en route* to Highbridge with a couple of Ivatt Class 2MT 2-6-2T engines in charge, Nos.41283 and 41249. From Highbridge the special ran to Mangotsfield via Bristol behind Bulleid Light Pacific No.34013 *Okehampton* and was diesel hauled for the brief run from Mangotsfield to Bath (Green Park). On arrival at Bath *Okehampton* was joined by No.34057 *Biggin Hill* and the pair, hauling the *very last* southbound passenger train over the legendary S&D route, set off in the gathering gloom. Once they had passed a section of wrong line working at Radstock the two Bulleids reportedly gave an unforgettable, sparkling performance, apparently topping Masbury summit at record speed which, hopefully, at least did something to relieve the sombre mood on board the train. The special later returned to London from Templecombe with 'Merchant Navy' Class No.35028 *Clan Line* once again in charge. Presumably the Pacific spent the day simmering on Templecombe shed where it may have been an unprecedented sight. *Trevor Owen*

The Somerset & Dorset Line – 1862 to 1966. LMSR Class 8F 2-8-0 No.48706 and BR Standard Class 4MT 2-6-4T No.80043 'blow off' gently in Platform One after arrival with the SLS special from Bournemouth on the evening of 6th March. A wreath on the smokebox door and two small unofficial headboards decorate the front end of the Class 8F. This was the last passenger train to enter Green Park station and one wonders what was in the thoughts of those who were present to witness the end of this quite outstanding route that was held in such great affection by so many people. The S&D was steam operated until closure so it was perhaps ironic that the last passenger movement of all was that of the DMU returning to Birmingham. Part of this train is just visible in the other platform. Shortly after this shot was taken the DMU departed, the stock of the special was removed and the two steam locomotives retired to Green Park shed for the last time. The S&D was no more. *Trevor Owen*

6TH MARCH 1966 – THE LAST DAY OF OPERATION